THE LONELINESS OF MAN

RAYMOND
CHAPMAN

FORTRESS PRESS   PHILADELPHIA

Library of Congress Catalog Card Number 63-19548

© SCM PRESS LTD 1963
FIRST PUBLISHED 1963

Printed in U.S.A.

UB956   6532-J63

CONTENTS

PREFACE

It is no new discovery that loneliness is a particular problem of our time. The big towns foster it; technological advances give it nourishment; those things which seem to improve human life take their price in the increase of loneliness.

Psychologists and social workers do all that they can to alleviate the loneliness that becomes intolerable. Nothing that is said in the following pages should be thought to derogate in any way from what they are doing; for nothing indeed may ever be said against works of compassion. The special studies which have been made of particular aspects of loneliness and its causes are most valuable, and it is something which needs attention from the experts in every field of social studies and human relations.

Yet I believe that we err in regarding loneliness as something which can be completely cured. I have attempted to regard it as a factor in our human condition which is not to be treated as a weakness or abnormality. The sense of loneliness does not come from instability, or inadequacy, or failure to cope with life. It is inherent in what we are; and this book is written out of a faith which tells me that we are really something strange and wonderful. That which seems too often to be a wretched misfortune may turn out to be our glory.

What I have written here is not a clinical study. It is a product of experience, and owes its being to the countless people who have been willing to share their loneliness with my own. In particular I have learnt a great deal from the succession of students at Passfield Hall of the London School of Economics during the eleven years that I was there. We were a happy community, and loneliness was seldom present in its more obvious forms. However, there were conversations which revealed, in many unexpected ways, their moments of truth.

1

LONELY MAN

PEOPLE have often thought that human life is like a journey. Some, like John Bunyan in *The Pilgrim's Progress*, have written a story of how the hero sets out on his travels and meets all kinds of adventures, good and bad, before he comes to his happy rest. Though the nature of the destination may depend on the belief with which you start, the image of the journey has been found appropriate in many different cultures. There are all kinds of roads: some are clean and broad, thronged with people confidently following the same direction; others twist their rough and muddy way through dark hollows where no other foot seems ever to have trodden. The traveler may step out boldly for many miles, only to find himself suddenly lost as night is falling. There are pleasant inns along the way, where the lighted window promises food and rest, with talk and good fellowship to soothe the trials of the past day. But next morning we are soon at the crossroads again, and our new friends turn east while we turn west. Yes, life is very much like that.

I like best the image of the ship. No analogy is perfect, and it soon makes nonsense to try to find a parallel for every detail within one figure. Yet life at any given moment does resemble being a passenger on a ship that is far out from the land. A number of people are thrown into juxtaposition; few of them are together by previous choice, and those who have come in a family find that they are surrounded by new acquaintances with whom some kind of civil contact has to be made. They seem to be united by nothing more than physical proximity and the fact of all moving in the same direction at the same speed. Some of them seem to have duties connected with the progress of the ship. Their lives follow a pattern which requires them to be in certain places at certain times. Not all these are ever seen by the passengers; many of them work deep down inside the ship, seemingly cut off from the brighter life of sun and air, yet proving their importance by the fact that the ship continues to move. The passengers are a mixed crowd. Some of them seem to hate the sea and to be impatient to come to their journey's end. Others are thoroughly enjoying the trip and never worry about the time it will take or where the next port will be. Some spend all day on deck, happy in the unwonted gifts of open sky and clean air. Others are shut up in the saloon, playing cards or gossiping about the shore life that they have left behind.

When a solitary passenger climbs to the upper deck at night and stands looking at the white track astern or the unbroken horizon ahead, he may wonder what part he has in all this continual activity. He too has danced and drunk with the rest, has committed himself to the life that ebbs and flows on board like the sea itself. Yet how far has it touched him? He is not an exceptionally selfish man, but he knows that the importance of this voyage for him is simply that he is part of it. When it is over, he must follow his own way and none can say yet what that will be. Others will cross this same sea, will form their own temporary friendships and know their own anxieties and excitements. If the ship sinks on its next voyage, he will perhaps read about it and feel a special interest, a keener regret because something familiar has been lost. But it will not really touch him, will not be part of him like his present mild concern whether the breeze that cools him is going to blow up into something stronger. On the next voyage there may be a homicidal maniac on board; the ship may come upon an authentic sea serpent; he will be apart from it all.

He may accuse himself of callous indifference as he finds his thoughts running on in this way. Then he thinks how little it would matter to the passengers on the previous voyage if any of these things happened now to him. How little indeed it would touch his present associates if he now fell and disappeared under the waves forever. There would be regret, a shiver at the breakfast table next morning, but the voyage would go on. Yet for him it would have finished. For him ship, crew and passengers would have been annihilated as completely as if they and not he had perished. Death would end whatever he has learned to call reality. What might lie beyond is as closed to knowledge, as the sky is sealed against the waters all around him.

When these thoughts come to him, our traveler is probably alone. Quietly apart from the others, he finds an opportunity for reflection. But the loneliness which he discovers at this moment does not leave him when he returns to the light and noise below. Although he may not think of it again, although it may be blotted out by activity and company, something has been uncovered which will never again be completely hidden. If the great sea serpent does appear out of the night, its tentacles will pluck him as irrevocably into oblivion from his stool at the bar as from a solitary vigil in the crow's nest.

This kind of loneliness is not a physical state. It is not to be confused with the condition that may be called *aloneness*—not being in the company of other human beings. The problem of aloneness is indeed acute today, and in passing by it I do not want to suggest that it is of no importance. There has been, and still is, too much of the benevolence which concentrates on the metaphysics of a person's troubles and ignores the possibility of physical relief. It is a challenge for all who profess themselves Christians, and for all who profess a liberal humanism too, that old people should be alone for days on end without human communication; that the young who live and work in a big city should often find no companionship except from those whose delight is to exploit and degrade them; that there should be unexplained suicides in hotel bedrooms. In these things much is being done and much more remains to do. In striving here to do what is necessary, we are not touching the real problem of human loneliness, and it is as well that we should be aware of that fact. The potential dangers in many plans for society lie not in what they cover but in what their proponents believe that they cover. The state of being alone draws out and aggravates loneliness. It is what might be called a good "culture" for the germs of loneliness that live in every human being. Aloneness gives time for reflection, in which a man can understand that he is unique and can never fully communicate with others. Like our traveler on the ship, he knows that he has never seen reality except with himself at the center; the picture ceases to exist if his own consciousness is withdrawn from it. Yet he loves, he cares for those around him and for the plight of the whole human race. He tries not to live for himself alone, yet every natural indication seems to warn him that there is no escape from the walls of his own skull.

Aloneness is a state familiar enough in nature. The solitary pine on a distant ridge may inspire romantic feelings, but they are feelings not shared by the pine. Man's loneliness is not shared by any creature in the depths of the sea or above the line of the Himalayan snows. He may project his loneliness to the things of nature, finding images to comfort him or to formulate his despair, using the self-knowledge which is his prison. In *Pincher Martin* by William Golding—an important author to whom I shall return—the loneliness of the central character is of a different kind from the isolation of the rock on which the sea casts him. His physical aloneness brings out the selfishness and futility of his past life; he discovers his complete separation from decency only when the chance of communication with others has been taken away. The rock does not create his loneliness, but by holding him apart from human society it becomes the background against which his inner loneliness can at last reveal itself.

Aloneness may reveal and increase loneliness, but company does not cure it. We all know the frightening loneliness of the crowd, the worst of all because the customary screen has fallen. Nor does solitude necessarily increase loneliness. Those who share Hamlet's introspection and self-doubt may also share something of his self-sufficiency. "I could be bounded in a nutshell and count myself king of infinite space, were it not that I have bad dreams." Many of us might echo that, but the terror is not in the dream but in the awakening. Terror comes when self-limiting reality asserts itself, when everything and everybody external is seen as a shadow that cannot be grasped; a world of shades into which the too-substantial personality cannot enter.

Loneliness is the sight of purposeful activity in which one has no part. It is the busy street where people hurry because it matters to someone that they should reach their destinations. It is the party where all the other guests know each other and are eager to tell and to hear new things. Yet it is not always a standing apart. Loneliness is in the midst of friends, old comrades with whom one has drunk and laughed for years. In an instant the room is silent, and one looks into dead eyes that reflect no shared experience. It is on the top of a mountain where the mists suddenly divide to show the town so far below that people cannot possibly be living and moving in its tinyness. It is equally in the crowded train that stops inexplicably on a country line, grabbed out of time and suspended in another dimension while the birds sing outside in their freedom. Or that other train underground that is abandoned in the tunnel while the world goes on its way above and the doomed ones are left in "the growing terror of nothing to think about."[1] Loneliness is in the very acts of love, when the beloved becomes a stranger. It is in the moment of danger when life seems to hang as insubstantial as smoke over the parapet or under the iron wheels. It is in the newspaper headline that threatens destruction of everything that we have learned to know as the human condition. It is at the bed of death where love itself becomes a shell. And it is also in the moment of sacramental communion, where the body is no longer irksome but becomes for a moment the very means of receiving the divine. For this inescapable loneliness has its glory too. Christ must withdraw before his full glory is revealed, and no human aid breaks through the utter loneliness of the Cross.

The tube train is new, the mountain top is old; human loneliness transcends all considerations of time and place. The change is only in the external settings through which men must move and from which they may seek comfort and forgetfulness. Therefore every age must have

[1] T. S. Eliot, "East Coker."

its special problems, and yet the same problem. To deplore the total badness of the age in which one happens to live is at best a negative attitude, a kind of persecution-mania which paralyzes the will and stops the means of improving what is indeed bad. If we are to see a greater problem of loneliness in our own time, we must try to see it in relation to what has gone before. Our poets and philosophers offer us little comfort. They work through images of flight and panic, of desolation in the face of a universe that seems void of meaning. Paul Tillich sees us beset by the third of the "ontological fears": the fear of death in the ancient world, the fear of guilt that was strongest in the Middle Ages, and the fear of meaninglessness from which we now suffer.[2] Franz Kafka, the veritable prophet of *Angst*, gives us the whole treatment: the castle that dominates the countryside yet which gives no explanation of its authority; the trial for an offence that is never named; the desperate burrowing of a hunted creature that can find no escape.

If these are true symbols of our time, we naturally want to ask the eternal question, Why? What is there that makes us feel so especially helpless, desolate and unable to communicate? The answers come readily enough, and they have been called to blame for many things besides loneliness. The scapegoat is a creature that has to be changed from time to time. But if too many sins are loaded on its back during its brief and unwelcome period of office, this does not prevent it

[2] Paul Tillich, *The Courage to Be* (New Haven: 1952), pp. 40-57.

from bearing a few genuine sins of its own. However often the words are repeated, it remains true that we live in a highly self-conscious and analytical age. We are constantly reminded of our difficulties and told that we are anxious, lost and introspective. We are also told on all sides that we live in a fragmented society where there is no common background of belief from which valid symbols can be drawn. It is a society in which home ties and local affiliations are weakened, so that there is more of the physical aloneness which draws out inner loneliness. Work is often impersonal and boring, the service of a big, anonymous corporation with no visible representative to be loved or hated. In two generations we have seen terrible wars and their consequences, a reversion to studied barbarity which we thought the human race had long outgrown. We have seen allies turned into potential enemies, and old enemies wooed for their prosperity. In the midst of it all we stand amazed and question whether any loyalty endures, whether there is anything of which people are not capable in the ways of hatred, vanity and mutual destruction.

All these things we know; and the worst of it is that we know ourselves to be a part of the situation. Hopelessly involved in the march toward annihilation, we know that this same annihilation is one way of bringing about the individual death which each one of us must meet. The shadow that hovers in its mushroom shape above the world is just one visual symbol of what nobody can escape. It is as important to us, in this our time, as the personification of pestilence and famine were to earlier ages. The forms differ, but that which they bring is the same. Whoever looks on these forms cannot see beyond them, for there lies his own extinction. And after that, the world will cease to exist for him. Even the Christian faith in resurrection after bodily death offers no other gateway but the oblivion of the flesh, and gives no special details of what is to come.

Are these thoughts only for the readers of Tillich and Kafka? Is this lonely anxiety a rarefied indulgence for those who have too much time left free for introspection? Do young people already believe that Hiroshima and Nagasaki touched only others, never themselves? Hear the terrible words of a youth sentenced to death, already close to the final loneliness. "They used to tell me that I'd be hanged, but what the hell. If the noose don't get you, the H-bomb will." [3]

[3] Newspaper report of the words of Victor Terry, hanged on 25 May 1961.

2

YOU TAKE YOUR CHOICE

THE READER has by now been brought to a state of gloom and general depression and is probably wondering why books should be written to emphasize the troubles which life already makes too obvious. If he feels that we have reached the bottom of the abyss, so much the better; for it is a point from which the only exit is to climb bravely upward. I hope to show that, in looking squarely at the anxiety of loneliness, we are going to conquer it. These factors which seem to lead to despair and nihilism may turn out to be the beginning of the greatest hope mankind can have. Christianity was founded in loneliness and loss.

But let us pause for a moment. If the depressed reader looks out of the window, he will soon be brought back from the dark visions with which the first chapter ended. People are there, people warm and living like himself, with whom he can communicate by the agreed rules of language. They are moving to and fro, each bent on some purpose that is absorbing all his attention. Traffic rushes past, proclaiming man's control over the natural world. If it is a quieter street outside, perhaps there will be children playing, or a tradesman making his leisurely round; the family, the guardian of life, must and shall go on. If it is night, or the house is very remote, a turn of the TV knob or a glance at the newspaper will bring evidence that no one need be alone. A great number of people are making it their special business to stimulate, to entertain, or pleasurably to shock. The consumer is always right; all is designed for his satisfaction.

Which then is the true world? Once a man has stood alone on the deck and realized his utter loneliness, must he always turn his back on all activities? Is it all false— the search for amusement, the cycles of commerce, the progress of technology, even the unselfishness of parental love? Is it all simply an escape from a greater reality? Some have thought that it is. The vision of loneliness can be a blinding one, and some of the greatest minds have retreated from the everyday world in an effort to find again the reality which has been glimpsed for a moment. Then every activity seems futile, a mere palliation of the grim truth. Such was the reaction which Tolstoy expressed through one of his characters:

> Sometimes he remembered how he had heard that soldiers in war when entrenched under the enemy's fire, if they have nothing to do, try hard to find some occupation the more easily to bear the danger. . . . All men seemed like those soldiers, seeking refuge from life: some in ambition, some in cards, some in framing laws, some in women, some in toys, some in horses, some in politics, some in sport, some in wine and some in governmental affairs. "Nothing is trivial and nothing is important, it's all the same—only

to save oneself from it as best one can . . . only not to see *it*, that dreadful it." [1]

Is that indeed the answer to all our hopes? If everything external is to be condemned as false, we may seem to be left with very little that makes life worth having. To delve deeper and deeper into the self is a drastic remedy for loneliness, yet some thinkers believe that it is the only one. Man, they say, never knows himself as he is until he is able to throw away all that gives him comfort and security. His authentic being is not in the warm saloon, not even on the protection of the quiet deck, but out on the raging sea alone. It is a thought that has found expression many times. Pascal, who three hundred years ago, saw the tragic loneliness of existence— the *"dreadful it"*—also tried to steer men away from external appearances:

> Now the order of thought is to begin with self, the author of our being, and our latter end. But what does the world think about? Never of these things; but of dancing, playing the lute, singing, making verses, running at the ring, of fighting, being made king without thinking what it is to be a king and what to be a man. [2]

Thirteen hundred years before Pascal, St. Augustine could look back on his youth and see how he had long been kept from the knowledge of God by "the vanity of popular fame, the plaudits of the theater, the quickly-fading crown awarded in the poetic contests." [3] Nor

[1] Leo Tolstoy, *War and Peace.*

[2] Blaise Pascal, *Thoughts*, selected and translated by M. Kaufman (Cambridge: 1908), p. 92.

[3] St. Augustine, *Confessions*, IV. 1. i.

is it only Christian asceticism that sees vanity in those things which delight the multitude. The road to all kinds of private gods leads away from the ordinary round and he who treads it is no less conscious of man's plight:

> We are all *condamnés*, as Victor Hugo says: we are all under sentence of death but with a thought of infinite reprieve . . . we have an interval, and then our place knows us no more. Some spend this interval in listlessness, some in high passions, the wisest, at least among "the children of this world," in art and song.[4]

You take your choice. That is what emerges from being confronted with our own loneliness. Must we say that, whatever choice is made, it will be ultimately meaningless? Is any choice as good, or as bad as another? In this state of crisis, do words like good and bad cease to have any meaning? Such conclusions have indeed been reached, but I do not believe that they are implicit in the situation that we are trying to meet. I believe instead that the situation makes choice significant and itself points to how we ought to choose. Human activity has not lost its meaning. But the purpose of activity, the very dignity of the human being who chooses to act, may be lost in the scramble to escape from loneliness. If something is undertaken in order to cover up what we want to forget, it will fail in that purpose and may also lose what is intrinsically good in itself.

[4] Walter Pater, "Conclusion" to *The Renaissance* (1868); omitted in the second edition, because Pater "conceived it might possibly mislead some of those young men into whose hands it might fall."

Here the reader may be moved to protest again. Having been led into the abyss and then promised a clue to the way out, he now feels that he is being pushed back while every rope is pulled out of sight. "Why should we not find what comfort we can in activities which are pleasant and harmless? They may not be good enough for Tolstoy and Pascal, but they are delightful and rewarding for those who undertake them instead of condemning them from a distance. What is wrong with a bit of good old escapism?" And those who like to answer imagery with imagery may say, "We know well enough that the little fire in the hearth has no effect on the cold night outside. Because the frost is heavy and reaches to our very windows, must we put out the fire and expose our home to the cold? You would seem to say that the fire is useless because it is a palliative against the weather which we cannot control."

No, let your fire burn brightly. You lit it because you knew that the night around your home was cold and dark. The warm room gets its meaning from the contrast with what lies all around it. Folly and futility would come only if you pretended that the air outside was warm; what need for your fire, unless you accept the surrounding cold? If you thought that, by lighting a fire in one room, you would banish all darkness and cold from the universe, then you would be like those whom the philosophers condemn. Or if you pretended that you could stay forever in that one warm room, never going out into the cold and darkness—that would be escapism of the worst kind, and the shock of departure would be the worse for it. It is this kind of make-believe that is practiced by those who hope to find a permanent outward refuge from inward loneliness. Happiness and comfort are not to be condemned: nor are they to be deified.

You take your choice. The philosophy that starts from awareness of man's lonely state ends by asserting the importance of his choice. Readers whose digestion is troubled by either or both of the words "philosophy" and "existentialist" may now exercise their right of choice and miss a paragraph or two. I hope that they will not, for existentialist philosophy has a wide influence today; it is a way of thinking which may help to unravel some of the problems which have been piling up in the last few pages. And it bears an attitude to the lonely individual which in itself gives some of the comfort that we have decided not to refuse.

Most people perhaps, when they hear of existentialism, think of the philosophy and plays of Jean-Paul Sartre. They have very likely been repelled by the apparent excesses of despair and the "do as you please" type of behavior which was associated with the so-called existentialist clubs and groups both here and in France a few years ago. Sartre, like many another thinker, is not to be blamed for the faults of his disciples (and all through history people have distorted philosophy as an excuse for doing as they pleased). He is only one of many philosophers whose way of thinking can be described as existentialist. The list has sometimes been extended back to include such improbable yokefellows as Coleridge, Pascal and St. Thomas Aquinas. More recently, it may certainly include Kirkegaard, Jaspers, Heidegger, Marcel and Sartre—and these are by no means all. Christians and atheists are thrust together—what have they in common that they should bear this title?

The existentialist believes that all begins with the individual, who is unique. Reality is the situation of an individual human being. Vague "essences" or qualities which have no embodied form are not open to consideration. Meaningful statements can be made only about that which exists in a distinct form. The whole tendency of existentialism is therefore away from abstract speculation and "toward concreteness and adequacy." Its concern is not with what might be in the realm of fancy, but with what will in fact be effective in a given situation. Terms like "metaphysics" and "pure thought," which had come to be regarded by many as the business of philosophy, have no significance beside the problems and potentialities of individual existence. Thought itself is valid only as part of the thinker's experience within his situation; and only from that experience can the truth of any proposition be examined.

By its concern with the individual, existentialism faces the problems of the age. It is a philosophy of crisis, offering no calm retreat from the dust of conflict. It is concerned with the very conflicts and tensions within people who must live their lives today; it does not shrink from the challenge of anxiety, loneliness and death. It recognizes, too, the paradox in the human condition. For each one of us, unique and individual, is yet involved in the whole situation of the race. Man is complete, "authentic," when he accepts his involvement; he is born not to be a detached observer but to be passionate, "in process of becoming." Thus he must continually exercise choice: it is a privilege and a duty which his very individuality lays upon him. His use of free choice within a situation is his true existence as an individual. Even if he refuses to choose, that refusal is still a choice.

Here, then, is a possible answer to the question of how we may continue to live fully in the world while recognizing that no activity has ultimate significance. Committed and conscious choice within the situation may be the assertion of lasting values. Before we can look at this within the Christian perspective, however, there are other roads to be traveled—and some of them seem at first to offer the most pleasing scenery. Existentialism itself can easily turn into a dark road, leading to the void in which nothing matters. An honest recognition of the individual's loneliness, of his unique situation, can result in the idea that he is beyond help, beyond praise or blame for his actions. Yet we have been forced to accept this loneliness. Can it be turned into hope, perhaps into the greatest hope? One great Christian existentialist thought that it could when, using once more the imagery of the sea, he declared that to be "in danger, above seventy fathoms of water, many miles from all help, there to be joyful—that is great." [5]

There to be joyful: that is what the individual may

[5] Søren Kierkegaard, *For Self-Examination* (1851).

choose to be. Thus we are constantly brought back to the importance of choice, made in an actual situation, in full awareness of that situation and thus transforming it. The act of choice must be made at some point which can then be called "the present," yet it is seldom if ever possible to take a stop watch and record suddenly, "Now I choose." The individual is made by all that impinges on him: his ancestry, past history, his own environment from birth onward, his friends, the books he has read and so on. An individual cannot be removed, by his own will or by any other force, from his situation; for his reality is himself within his situation at any given moment.

Now our exploration has brought us to a Christian statement, and an important one. Many discussions have taught me that one of the regular arguments against Christianity is that it destroys free choice. People seem to think that a Christian belongs to a club for which he has paid a life-membership fee, on the understanding that he will never again be troubled to make up his own mind about anything. The uniformed servants of the club will look at the rules and then tell him exactly what to do in every situation. In fact, a Christian is continually being required to choose. It is true that his membership is for life, and beyond, but he is not released for a moment from the responsibility for individual decision. One of the ways in which the whole outlook changes after accepting Christianity in adult life is that free choice is seen to be more important than one had ever supposed. Every action now shows antecedents and consequences that had never even given a hint of their existence. God's working through the apparently trivial and commonplace is understood. Indeed, Christians are sometimes so overwhelmed by the implications of choice that they develop what are known as "scruples" and get into states of anxiety that have to be dispelled by wise counsel. Then the opposition, never at a loss for points of attack, can accuse Christians of being excessively fussy over small details of conduct, and the next moment say that they do not bother to decide anything for themselves.

If everybody who argued about Christianity would start from Christian foundations, the issues might be made clearer and a great deal of time and breath saved. Both Christians and unbelievers often fail to do so. The New Testament is packed full of individual choices. The kerygma, the gospel message, rings out as a clarion demand for choice. The choice is to be made whenever it is offered, and however, by the individual in his own situation. The disciples were called straight from their daily occupations of fishing or collecting taxes. Every word of Christ went directly to the individual need and demanded an individual response. The popular and well-loved figure of the Good Shepherd has had some unfortunate results. It is easy to forget the symbol of wise and loving protection, and to think only of the woolly crowd of sheep that run all in one direction, without choice or understanding. But we are not called to run all one way; or rather, we are called to the same destination but are given routes of different length and difficulty

for getting there. Christ did not require the whole population of Palestine to follow him on the road to Jerusalem,
any more than he has now limited salvation to priests
and monks. The rich man was called to abandon his
wealth and follow; the healed demoniac was told to go
quietly back to ordinary life, and not to start shouting
about what had happened to him. The right choice was
shown to them, but each was left free to choose whether
to follow it. Christian choice requires a positive, not a
negative, state of the will. He who understood the par-
able of the Good Samaritan was then told, "Go, and do
thou likewise." Christ commands, does not compel;
neither the rich man nor the demoniac obeyed him.

Christ continues to make the supreme claim which
allows no compromise. The "liberal" Christ, the
"modern" Christ, the "Jesus of history behind the
Gospels," bear little resemblance to the Christ of Christianity. A little advice on how to behave, from a teacher
made safe and respectable by death and history, is not
too irksome. It may give some weight to what we already
intend to do; if not it can easily be ignored, for any
teacher may be mistaken. Times change, we must move
with the times, and so on. But when a man says, "I am
the Way, the Truth and the Life: no man cometh unto
the Father but by Me"; when he blesses the follower
who blurts out the confession, "Thou art the Christ, the
Son of the living God"; when the very teaching is given
to the world deep-rooted in the belief that this man has
been seen to triumph over death and to be made free of
natural laws—that is a different matter. These are the

claims which everyone has to consider, in his own place and generation. Choice is demanded for Herod or for Joseph, to reject or to honor the divinity that is come into the world.

Now the atheist must snort. Why do these Christians spoil a set of precepts which on the whole are perfectly sound, by handing them on in this peculiar way? They dishonor a great man, one might say a great humanist, by asserting that he was not an ordinary man at all, but that he "came down" and "rose up" as if there were a heaven spatially above this earth. Why must they use this fairy-tale language? The answer is simple: because there is no reliable record of Christ's teaching except in relation to his Person. Those who recorded and preached his words did so in the faith of his resurrection. If they were mistaken in one way, why give them credence in another? There are no half-portions here. You take your choice.

The atheist snorts again—only by now he has started to call himself an agnostic. "I deny your assumption that I must choose. I will not make any decision on insufficient evidence. These things are not within the scope of that which is humanly knowable." Very well: but that refusal is itself a choice, based on a voluntary attitude toward what constitutes evidence. Christianity asserts that all we need to know about transcendental God can be, and has been, revealed in immanent, this-worldly terms. Human language, inadequate as it is, has been empowered to transmit eternal truth. Human nature, unworthy as it is, has yet been taken into the divine nature. The agnostic's refusal, however he may express it, is absolute and not conditional. And indeed there is no other kind of refusal or acceptance which is either required or permitted.

Every creed, religious or secular, demands that he who professes it shall have the honesty and courage to accept the logical consequences. Every personal relationship demands the same thing, whether it be a relationship of love or of hate, whether it be sanctified or illicit. Because man's natural perception and common sense often exceeds his courage, he will make frantic efforts to avoid choosing or to pretend that he has not chosen. The fear of choice goes deep today, and might perhaps add a fourth to Tillich's three "ontological fears." People will use a great deal of mental and nervous energy in avoiding a decision. Lonely man encounters dread when he realizes that he is making himself by his choices. The more deeply he is committed, the more involved in the total situation, then the more is choice demanded of him. Of all commitments, Christianity makes the heaviest demands. It is no wonder that the sub-Christian fringe makes use of spirit-guides and oracles, or searches for a text that will make all plain. And sometimes once again the refuge is in flight, in the assertion that free choice is not possible.

There is no arguing with the complete determinist. If everything is predestined from the first confluence of molecules in the universe, nobody is able to choose his arguments or change his mind. There is no point in discussion if the opposing sides were settled before those who discuss were born. No, we must look more honestly at our loneliness, believing that whoever suffers it has also the power of free choice. Can we then hope to find any means of judging the many choices that are made? For we find that the flight from loneliness takes men off in many directions. Something may be learned by following a few of them and looking with clear eyes at what lies ahead. There will turn out to be many visions that cannot bear the light of reality. Men may travel toward paradises that they themselves have created. And there are many ways that lead to good, but not to the greatest good. Society today may seem to offer an abundance of choices by which we can escape from dread, from the loneliness of being out over seventy fathoms, from the dreadful *it*. But fear has a way of walking beside us, unseen until the moment when other companions fall away and we have to face it alone.

What about the Christian hope, which asserts that there is indeed a paradise, not of our own making but offered freely to us? The only way of finding out is to tread the way that leads to it. Do not be surprised if the road to that paradise turns out to be different from your expectations of it. Christians and tentative inquirers have found that it does not correspond with the pictures of it on the walls of Sunday schools, nor to the word-pictures of the dear old rationalist pamphlets. It is a road of contradictions and paradoxes, of suffering without despair, of desolation that is full of hope. The traveler may find himself, "as unknown, and yet well known; as dying, and behold we live; as chastened, and not killed; as sorrowful, yet always rejoicing; as poor, yet making many rich; as having nothing, and yet possessing all things." [6] Travelers who have seen what lies at the end of the road often find it hard to describe. They seem to agree, however, that it is something very lively, that it is in fact Life, to a degree that makes our own idea of living seem like death. It is certainly not a road to be taken if you are fond of sleep; or if you dislike making decisions. For this Life is not a vague power that we can draw on or leave alone. Misleading though the word may be in some respects, the Life that accompanies us and draws us onward can best be thought of as a Person. All that is personal to each of us is known, even the loneliness.

[6] II Corinthians 6:9.

3

AND YOU PAY YOUR
MONEY

THERE IS one symptom of the dread of loneliness which
had better be cleared out of the way before we turn to
others that deserve more serious consideration. I mean
the way in which loneliness and the resultant wish for
belonging are exploited for commercial purposes: the
insidious appeal of advertisements and the enterprises
which claim to be "clubs" or "circles." The invitation
to belong which is given in this way is wholly bad,
because it is based on payment in money. Nothing is
given except as a return for cash. Now it may be thought
that this is fair enough, in a society which runs its
economy, and bases many of its cultural and social values,
on money. I have no wish to disrupt the nation's
economy by abolishing money. I have found it very
useful stuff; further, I have no competence to suggest
what could take its place or how a system of barter could
be worked in the modern world. But this exploitation
of the wish for belonging is bad, because it offers for
money something which money can never buy. Money
can to some extent solve the problem of aloneness. It

can buy company, but we have already seen that mere juxtaposition does not solve the loneliness of the individual, is not even relevant to it. It is, however, worth remembering that even the company of others bent on a common purpose is not easily obtained today without money. A static crowd usually has its price; it is only the featureless, ever-moving crowd of the streets and open spaces that is free to all.

The firms which offer the incentives of "membership" are to be condemned for it. They are cashing in on human loneliness. They would not put it in those terms, even in their own inner conclaves, but that is what they are doing. They would no doubt say in their defence that there is a known need and they are trying to meet it; business is business. But human loneliness is not business. A specific desire to join something can be met, but there is no refuge to be bought from the fear of one's own uniqueness, of being cut off from communication with others because of an essential difference. The difference is the personality; it is to be faced and accepted, before any transaction becomes worth while. The commercial planners are right if they say that there is a need; and we need not argue with them if they say that they *seem* to meet it, instead of claiming that they actually do so. The appeal is successful in selling the goods. It answers to a longing that is specially great at this time, and that is why it is important. People are naturally told what they want to hear, for irritated and anxious people are not good customers. At one time you could sell your wares in the market place by saying that they had been blessed by a dignitary of the church. Today you can sell them through the newspapers by saying, however subtly, that they will stop you from feeling lonely. Each age will have its own image of what it wants. Nobody tells you that, if you buy a certain product, you will then be left in peace to enjoy its intrinsic merits.

It is interesting to see how few advertisements now confine themselves to claiming that the product will do the job for which the buyer is paying its manufacturer. More often, the purchase and use of the product is associated with other kinds of felicity, quite irrelevant to the supposed purpose. Most absurd are the advertisements which inform you that the mere possession and use of the product will cause you to have friends. We may see here how the advertising expert works—and it is a process that deserves some thought for its reflection of wider present-day issues. The first stage is an axiom which nearly everybody holds, an axiom not proved by experiment but perhaps roughly tested by a few experiences. This axiom is then taken and thrust before the consumer, coupled with the name of a particular product. The offering of a cigarette is a friendly gesture and helps to establish a quicker sympathy at a first meeting: such a brand of cigarette is the most certain to produce this result: therefore if you smoke and offer this brand you will make more friends than those who do not. Not being personally clean makes you repulsive to most other people in this country today: this brand of soap (or deodorant—supreme hypocrisy) will make you seem cleaner than any other: therefore no one will shun your company, and you will be the center of attraction. A variant approach is the type of advertisement where a famous "personality"—the modern use of that word is worth pondering too—gives his or her approval to the particular brand. The "personality's" competence to give any opinion on this matter has to be accepted as an unchallenged assumption. He is a famous character, popular, glamorous; emulation in the choice of toothpaste, hair cream, writing paper, ink, cough mixture or anything else will turn the consumer into a creature of fame, popularity and glamour. Truly, we live in an age of faith!

My purpose is not to condemn advertising and advertisers. This commercial publicity has become a business in itself now, and those who are engaged in it are no doubt mostly admirable citizens, honest in their private dealings and devoted to their families. Very likely they suffer their own particular loneliness as individuals. Yet there is a word more to be said, if we are to understand the wider situation which is now our concern. A more subtle type of approach through the advertisement does not suggest quite so blatantly that using the product will give you all that you want from life. Sometimes the users of the product are shown, pictorially or verbally, in the company of others: you come to be the sort of person who has plenty of friends. The surroundings are always comfortable and "gracious." You are not drinking the gin together out of cracked cups, or making coffee for a group of friends sitting around on soapboxes.

Everything will improve if you shop wisely. Not to improve out of all recognition: people are not so stupid as to be taken in by that. No, the situation in the advertisement is nearly always the one that would be just attainable through a good promotion, or a lucky win, but not one that would put the whole family out of its depth. The association of named brands with prosperity and company is reminiscent of the old lectures on total abstinence which used to be given with lantern slides, and which may still be seen in a briefer form in some old-fashioned almanacs. The drunkard who signs the pledge is transformed not into the respectable working-man that he was before he started drinking, but into a pompous figure in a frock coat and top hat.

So even the favorite snob appeal is combined with the appeal to belonging. Why is it so important to become a Top Person? Because there are other Top People, and you will get on well with them and no longer feel lonely. It is instructive to see the comparatively recent changes in advertising methods in this respect. The goal of promotion, and the social status that goes with it, is not so often shown as the power to command and take decisions independently of others. It is rather to meet nicer people, people who will appreciate and understand. The symbol of success is no longer the mansion on a hill but the more spacious drawing room for entertaining more gracious people. This is one of the imagined paradises. Somewhere there must be people who are not insecure and lonely. We catch glimpses of them sometimes, as they step from their cars or pass through the doors of a big hotel. They seem to be perfectly at ease, never alone, always full of pleasure. It is only money that keeps us from being one of them. That is the kind of logic that runs through many minds, and which the advertisements reflect. The desire to escape from the known social group is not caused by active dislike of the group itself, or of group life in general, but by the lure of a higher group which offers fuller integration. The self has known anxiety and loneliness, and has known them in the environment of one part only of society. It is natural, but mistaken, to suppose that freedom from the environment will mean freedom from all the unwelcome things that are experienced within it. This is a very old fallacy: those who rush overseas may change the sky above but not their own souls.[1] The commercial possibilities of the fallacy are only now being realized.

These are comparatively subtle approaches to the loneliness that engenders a wish for belonging. While these advertisers lead the buyer gently through conformity to participation and ultimately to fellowship, others thrust him headlong into a "club." The majority of these "clubs" are conducted through post-office box numbers, where the firm is at a safe distance from the cares or delights of "membership." There is nothing new about this either, only about the approach which is used. Christmas clubs have been run by shops for many years, beginning from the last days of summer if not earlier.

[1] Horace, *Epistles*, xi. 27: *Caelum non animum mutant qui trans mare currunt.*

When I was a boy, I was a willing contributor to a fireworks club, in the days when a loud bang was a signal of jollity and not of disaster. But there never used to be any assumption, on either side of the counter, that these were anything more than a convenient method of weekly saving, with perhaps a small bonus at the end as an incentive to pledge one's custom to a single shop. The ethos of the modern mail-order "club" is different. It holds out promises of fellowship and friendship. The lonely soul who starts a group or branch will soon be taken to the hearts of all who join. From a solitary bed-sitting room, he or she is transported to a round of dances, coach trips and general *bonhomie*. A likely story, when the business of the organizer is to extract weekly payments for goods already delivered and in use. One could think of surer ways of becoming the most popular person in the street. The rewards here offered are humbler and more immediately accessible than those in the big national advertisements. It is not suggested that you will find yourself in a different stratum of society, but that you will be fully integrated in the known environment.

Nevertheless, the implications are as interesting and as dangerous as those of the more extravagant claims. They are worth examining, not as a condemnation of the "club" but as a guide to how people are motivated. First, we see that here too there is the presupposition of an existing society that is integrated, free from care and dread. Most other people are happy, protected from loneliness by many wonderful friends. The reader of the advertisement is made to identify him or herself with the lonely one, who is presented as an attractive and sensitive person. Only the magic key is lacking to give that person his or her rightful place. It is the old story of the youngest son, the handsome swineherd, the brave little tailor. The most attractive fantasies are those in which we see ourselves as victims of circumstances and dream of the time when our true qualities will be recognized.

These fantasies compel belief in a happier state which is just out of reach but not unattainable. It is no good dreaming about promotion if the firm is entirely composed of junior clerks, and you can't rent a higher room if you are already living on the roof. In this instance, paradise is a place where people are not lonely. Loneliness is seen as something remediable, something peculiar and outside the normal human lot, which can be changed by circumstances alone. People do not see, and do not want to know, that their loneliness is within them. To trade on loneliness and the need of belonging, assigning false causes and promising a remedy by external means, is wholly bad.

Morally speaking, one of the greatest dangers is that this mentality often leads to the sin of envy. Nobody needs the aid of moral theology to tell him that envy is a deadly sin. We all know too well the effects of it in our own and others' lives—how it spreads from one small item of discontent through the whole person, poisoning even the pleasures which it ought not to be able to touch. Sexual jealousy runs through the history of civilized man, in all degrees from the passion of Othello to the latest sordid little quarrel at the garden gate. Envy of happiness which others seem to possess is even stronger and more evil. Othello murders for misplaced love and a lack of faith, but he retains the hero's greatness. Iago, the utter villain, is driven on by rankling disappointment about promotion and bitterness at the joy which others seem to have. "He hath a daily beauty in his life, that makes me ugly." That is how he looks at Cassio, and that indeed is the envy of those who mistake their inner loneliness for a lack of proper recognition. Envy turns its bearer in on himself, increases his isolation and thus gives loneliness a better breeding ground. It can turn a rational adult into a child who won't play and wants to upset those who do.

A stage beyond envy is despair, the ultimate sin. The will becomes atrophied and cannot consent even to evil-doing. Despair can come from many causes: from long sickness, from poverty which gives no release from the mere business of keeping alive, from the continual triumph of forces known to be wrong. There is also the despair which steals over a person who continues to believe in the beatific vision but fears that it is unattainable. Self-doubt can play some strange tricks, turning the essential virtue of humility into a wilderness of fear. It is a problem all too common in Christian life: once again the question of "scruples" but now carried to a tragic conclusion. The certainty of damnation is perhaps the most terrible fear that can afflict a man. Its torments can be approached, never fully shared, by reading Bunyan's *Grace Abounding;* it afflicted many others, particularly in that period and the century which fol-

lowed. Also, it is too well known that many who pro-
fessed to teach Christianity taught in fact a message of
fear and despair. But what when this despair is suffered
not from a perversion of that which remains true in
spite of it, but from a belief in something that never
did and never could exist? Yet people are being made
profoundly miserable every day by the thought that
they are marked out specially for loneliness, cut off
from the company of those who know no such thing.

There ought to be a few words here on the football
pool approach, though we are now near to absurdity.
It may be wondered whether anybody at all can take
seriously the protestations of goodwill and fellowship
from those whose comfortable living depends on people
losing money by gambling. Presumably they do, for
the pools promoters are too shrewd to harm themselves
by a bit of misapplied psychology. So the gambler is
made to feel that he belongs, that he and others—millions
of others—are members of a friendly circle. The devices
for making them believe this vary from one company to
another. Some receive a membership card which they
are asked to sign. A "personal message" from the
managing director is common; and though they may
be printed by the million, these slips of paper seem to
give the impression that there is Somebody who Cares.
The transition from this to the conviction that Big
Brother is watching you would not seem to present much
difficulty, a thought which the reader may care to
ponder during a sleepless night. At the time of writing,
even the supremacy of the football pools is being nibbled

at by the craze for bingo. This offers physical proximity
with other gamblers and allows the illusion of belonging
to be stoutly fostered. An advertisement for a bingo
center announces that "A member won £100 last week."
A form of belonging which rests on the hope of getting
money which other people lose, and the certainty of
making money for the organizer: this is not quite what
St. Paul meant by being "members one of another."

There is another approach, at once more flagrant and
more subtle. The last few years have seen a remarkable
growth in the number of "clubs" for books and gramophone records. This is in many ways an admirable thing.
It is good that so many more people should have the
interest, the leisure and the money to enjoy reading and
music. The economics of the deal seem to please everybody and to be entirely sensible. But it is not enough to
make it a straightforward business transaction. It might
be thought that people would be content with an offer
of goods at reduced prices, on the condition that a certain
minimum order was given over an agreed period. But
no, the bargain must be disguised in the garb of belonging. There must be something to "join" if the net is to
be cast to its fullest extent. It is not just those who will
pay the required sum who get the promised goods, but
"members" who are "privileged to receive" them. These
so-called clubs do not go quite so far as to ask for a
"membership fee" as well as the cost of the books or
records; but they often make great play with the fact
that "there is no membership fee or subscription." They
have been known, however, to levy "club dues" and

then proudly exclaim that "there is no charge for post, packing or insurance." Sometimes the personal approach wears rather thin, when it conflicts with administrative convenience. Every member has a number, which he is to give in all correspondence with the club. This does not sound like the sort of belonging which most people desire. There is a prison aura around it—give your name and number to the warden.

The great event of the month is the bulletin, journal or magazine which accompanies the book or record. This plays the membership theme very hard, sometimes with a nauseating stylistic mixture of coquetry and nursery bullying. Members are assured that they are really wonderful people, that the club loves to hear from them. Unfortunately, the club cannot enter into correspondence with members: in other words, letters will not be answered. In fact the club seems to be a curious entity. It is capable of likes and dislikes and is brimming over with benevolence, but like a corporation it has neither a body to be kicked nor a soul to be damned. It regards with lachrymose sorrow those who are unkind to it, keeping up the illusion of membership to the end. There are "rules," concerned mostly with the regular payment of money. Those who do not buy often enough are stigmatized as "inactive members" and threatened that they may be "asked to resign."

So there it is: business is business and presumably people on both sides of the counter like it that way. These organizations mostly give a worthwhile service, and not all are equally brash in their fostering of the

membership and belonging illusion. Some of them have
encouraged the formation of local groups where
"members" can be more like members, by meeting each
other to play records and discuss books. This is good,
though it is not the answer we are seeking. The point
of the present analysis is not to condemn those who
run these organizations, still less to ridicule those who
belong to them. It is to show how the need for group
membership, wrongly conceived as a refuge from loneliness, is widespread enough to become a commercial
proposition. Offers of belonging are found to be acceptable, even in the most improbable guise.

The group appeal is often strong in the advertisements for vacations, especially for organized tours and
holiday camps. To meet other people, to make "new
and exciting friendships," is presented as the major attraction of a holiday. The contacts which are made in
the agreeable but artificial conditions of a holiday are
notoriously short lived. The exchange of addresses
illuminated by the last flush of sun nearly always proves
to lack the roots of real friendship, based on long knowledge and delight in each other's company irrespective
of surroundings. Yet most of us, even seeing these things
to be true where they are set down on cold, autumnal
paper, forget them when summer returns. Too often
the time for refreshment of body and mind becomes a
time of fresh emulation, of over-appraisal of what other
people's ordinary lives are like. It becomes yet another
desperate attempt to escape from loneliness, for here
again is the image of paradise set before us. The camp,

tour or whatever it may be, is presented as a place where everyone is happy, where friendship blossoms and never a hard word is spoken. The sun shines continually, the days pass in the most delightful activities. No children are ever heard to cry, there is no sickness, no mosquitoes, no colds from unadvertised rain. In fact, it is rather like the more popular old-fashioned image of heaven itself. The only misfortune conceivable in relation to such a place is to be left outside it. But the lonely soul may enter and share in its delights, knowing loneliness no more—provided he can pay the necessary fee for admission.

We have seen several approaches to the individual who is aware of his loneliness and believes it to be curable by external factors. These approaches have in common the encouragement of this belief, by playing on the idea that loneliness is due to some fault in the person who suffers it. They treat it as an unnecessary burden that can be lifted. Further, they build the image of an ideal society, where loneliness does not exist. Loneliness can be removed by a change of circumstances, and this change can be effected by the payment of money. Other benefits, real or illusory, may be offered; but a sense of belonging is thrown in as an added incentive. If anyone really believes that the cheerful protestations of good fellowship are true, he need only try to get a share in the offered benefits without paying for them. There is no provision for "members" in this situation. Fair enough, for the rights of life, liberty and the pursuit of happiness are held also by the manufacturers of cig-

arettes and gramophone records, by holiday camp own-
ers and perhaps even by football pool promoters. If
release from loneliness could be bought for money it
would be a most unjust state of affairs, but it would be
in keeping with the way in which things are done today.
The fault lies not in taking money for goods and services but in promising, even by implication, a service
which no money can buy.

Is there anything which money cannot buy? It can
buy company, and if this leaves the essential loneliness
untouched must we say that there is no solution? Or
is there anything beyond the reach of money, any place
to which admission cannot be bought? To suggest that
the possession of wealth can be inadequate and even
dangerous has a strange sound in the modern world.
Yet it is a warning which we have heard many times
and have perhaps chosen to ignore as generations before
us have ignored it. From the lectern and the pulpit, in
smart churches, in gloomy corrugated-iron mission halls,
in school assemblies and college chapels the word has
been uttered, "A rich man shall hardly enter into the
Kingdom of Heaven." No payment of money is asked
or accepted for that entry. There is only one price,
and that is nothing else than the whole self, with its
strength and its weakness, its failures, its very loneliness.

Here is a reversal indeed of the world's ideas, of ideas
which are held unquestioningly by many who cannot
be accused of excessive avarice. When Christ comes to
seek for the lost ones, he does not seek out first the rich.
Not only are the rich not flattered, they are warned

that their way to salvation is more perilous than other
men's. No one is without hope, no one is turned away
if his desire is true, but the rich are told plainly that
their salvation needs a special grace. Without that to
pull them through they would never pass the exceed-
ingly narrow gap in the wall which their riches have
set up between them and God. They are like camels
padded out to twice their size with loads of treasure,
trying to squeeze through where only a man on foot
can pass. The warning is repeated again and again: the
rich man who fails to relieve distress while he lives learns
how to suffer after death; the man who is complacent
with his possessions all around him dies suddenly and
unprepared; the pleasures of wealth seal men's ears
against the joyful news of salvation. Nor was this only
the temporary teaching of a small band specially dedicated to poverty. The first Christian preachers repeated
the warnings, never attempting to win the favor of the
rich and powerful whose support might have seemed
so desirable. The approach was to the poorest and most
despised sections of the community, and if the rich
came into the church, it was not the church that was
honored by it. The rich were not congratulated, but
were advised to "weep and howl for your miseries that
shall come upon you." [2] This was a new kind of belonging, one that no gold could buy. To the man who
followed the fashion of the Roman Empire and thought
that even spiritual gifts were up for sale, the reply was
clear: "Thy money perish with thee, because thou hast

[2] James 5:1.

thought that the gift of God may be purchased with money."

So you pay your money; but what you get for it may not be all that was promised. You cannot buy your way out of loneliness, and you cannot buy your way into the true heaven. Perhaps those two negatives are going to lead us on to something positive.

4

ALL CLING TOGETHER

THERE WAS a time, and perhaps that time has not yet passed, when attendances at Sunday schools used to increase very noticeably as Whitsun approached. It was hard for the teachers to explain to their small charges that, although participation in the Whitsun treat depended on a certain number of Sunday attendances, it was not in order to go to the treat that they came to Sunday school. Something of the same impression is given by many of the advertisements offering jobs in factories and offices. The amenities provided for the lucky worker are described in detail, the actual duties of the job often being relegated to a few words at the end. It would seem as if all employers were benevolent paternalists, anxious to make their staffs into one happy family. They not only offer money in exchange for services; they promise to transform and satisfy every aspect of life.

This may look healthier than the blatant commercial exploitation of loneliness which we have just been considering. If a refuge from loneliness can be given in reward for service rather than in exchange for money,

there might seem no reason to look further. It is not
long since there was little care for the worker's welfare
when he was in a job, and none when he was out of it.
It was out of suffering, out of bitter and prolonged
struggles, that there came the canteens and the health
precautions which are now taken for granted. These
extra amenities may seem to call for unqualified rejoicing.
Is man's loneliness overcome at last, through the work
which he must do to maintain himself and his family?

If this question cannot be answered with a simple agreement, the value of much that is being done is not thereby
denied. Friendship, the feeling of community, shared
enjoyment, are their own good. But the existence of
one kind of good does not allow it to give itself airs
and pretend to be another kind of good. In all these
things, it is still only the externals of loneliness that are
being touched. The real question once again is—Why?
Why are these sports grounds laid out, these excursions
planned? Is it from love and care for the individual
himself or because he is part of something bigger and
extra-human? Is he let into the club because he wears
a label saying, I am Joe Bloggs, or because he wears one
saying, I work for Super Products?

The possession of these labels is important in modern
society. People like to write their own and stick them
on those they meet. They are found at the social party,
where the names are usually misheard on introduction
and forgotten immediately afterwards. Most people
get along well enough without the name, so long as
they can find out something which places their new

acquaintance in a category. "He is a producer on ITV" or "She writes books about bee keeping," and all is well; fear of the unknown is overcome by the neat little label which prevents another human being from appearing either as a mystery or as a person who loves and suffers, and might become a nuisance to other loving and suffering ones. The police keep elaborate records by which a criminal can be detected from the method, type and general marks of a crime. Other organizations have adopted similar methods, and can pick out a man whose observed characteristics make him suitable for some new project.

Now perhaps the reader thinks that too much is being demanded. Super Products cannot provide recreation for men who contribute nothing to super production, and a cocktail party is not the place for hearing confessions.[1] Exactly: we are dealing with groups where something is demanded and something given in return. By the laws of this world, more is given than history gives us any right to expect. Yet the fact remains that the individual is absorbed in the group, and his interests are subordinated to group interests. Not only direct manual labor with an end product, but even the advancement of knowledge through research is evaluated by its contribution to the impersonal whole. It is not only the business executive today who deserves the title "organization man."[2] Individual choice and initiative are dis-

[1] Although it could be, if the will were well disposed; cf. T. S. Eliot, *The Cocktail Party.*
[2] See the valuable study by William H. Whyte, *The Organization Man* (New York: Doubleday Anchor Books, 1956).

couraged; there is an image of the organization which must be stamped on all who work for it. And those that have not the mark of the Beast on their foreheads are cast out.

Yet for the ordinary worker, in business, industry or the professions, the total situation seems to be much better than it has been in the past. From a mixture of philanthropy, self-interest and compulsion, employers now do something about protecting the health and safety of their people and making the conditions of work more tolerable. Workers are allowed and indeed encouraged to talk over their problems with people who are actually paid by the employer for that purpose. Is this done for love of the individual or because the contented worker is the useful worker? Personnel officers are usually good and dedicated people, but their value depends on what is permitted to them by the firm. It is perhaps not right to question the motives when good is manifestly being done. Yet this good too often is offered as if it were a greater good. That which is proper within the factory may become doubtful and even sinister outside. Loyalty to the firm, a sense of pride in its achievements, these are very well; but they are not the whole life of man. To stand at strict attention is appropriate for the parade ground but not for the drink afterwards. Kneeling can be a very good posture in church and a very bad one at the cinema. The good of the organization may be the ill of the man who is supposed to be at home and off duty.

It is well known that this is an age with the urge to

conformity. People who refuse the duties of Christian life accept much more constricting pressures from other sources. The rows of identical houses that stretch through all our towns and outside them are good evidence. Men who no longer break off their conversation for the hour of prayer now insist on silence for the football results. It is still easy to find the densest concentration of people on a Sunday morning, but you must seek on the main roads and not in the churches. Mass communications in all media encourage people to dress alike, to buy the same products and to think along the same lines. The few, mostly young, who protest and refuse to conform, are looked upon as no good, irresponsible, probably disloyal to their country. Yet there is much merit in the beatnik and the rebel, if only because they give some guarantee that you cannot obliterate the features of all the people all the time. Cleanliness is a fine and desirable thing; but when for many people cleanliness becomes more than godliness there may be something to be said for a few unwashed. Hair that is uncombed by deliberate choice may be a corrective to the many heads of hair that are given careful attention because an advertisement has decreed a weekly ritual of shampoo and setting lotion. Those who surprise and shock their elders are doing no more than was done by some of their liveliest ancestors, whose outlook they would dismiss so contemptuously if they knew anything about it.

The Romantics tended to make too much of the Outsider, to praise withdrawal and anti-conformity as a good in itself. The Organization Age looks coldly on all who withdraw from its control. The large firm is like nothing so much as the nastier type of private school, distrusting and harrying the individual who seeks to lead some of his life apart from the majority. The most able and industrious, who give most to the organization and deserve the greater freedom off duty, are the most relentlessly pursued. Large American corporations arrange "wife programs," to draw a man's whole family into their orbit and influence even his leisure time with his family.[3]

We are well on the way to the nightmare of complete conformity and control which has haunted some of the greatest minds of the century. There may seem to be a big and safe gap between enforced community singing on an English train returning from Blackpool and the dreary "orgies" of Huxley's *Brave New World* or the compulsory two-way television screens of Orwell's *1984*. Yet the gap could be bridged by some of the technical means which already exist for controlling the human mind. The seeds of boredom and loss of endeavor are latent in all utopias; the inverted utopias of some modern writers show us how those seeds could grow monstrously.

People accept organization and take part cheerfully enough in the fun and games that are provided. Is not their enjoyment genuine? Probably it is. Is enjoyment forced and assumed for fear of ostracism if they do not take part? I do not believe that it is, for ordinary people are capable of quite heroic resistance to the mass, if they stand on a matter of deeply-felt principle. No, the

[3] Whyte, *op. cit.*, pp. 287 ff.

grim specter which has been hovering all this time over the innocent company picnic is a creature of another order.

The evil of business that infiltrates into every aspect of private life, the evil of all conformity that is induced by external pressures, is not so far removed after all from the evil described in the previous chapters. It is not what is offered, but what pretends to be offered. People do not want to be left out of group activities, because this would increase their natural sense of loneliness. That the loneliness is there within them, will always be there and cannot be taken away, is a truth that they have never been allowed to learn. The existence of group activities of one kind or another has been taken as a safeguard against loneliness. When loneliness begins to well up and make itself felt, there has always been the club, the pub, the dance, to which to run for a refuge. Group activities deal with loneliness as effectively as aspirin deals with a bad tooth. The pain may be silenced but the condition remains. No great harm lies in hiding loneliness for a time by exchanging it with the loneliness of others. The artificial embrace on the dance floor can briefly express a need as old as mankind; and can be ennobled by that very need. The sentimental words of a song can assault the loose hordes of loneliness and force them to take a shape that can be accepted and faced; for this is indeed one of the ways in which the greatest arts act upon us. Yet none can escape the long walk home, alone and lonely, except by turning to other means again which may hold off realization. The fear of being left outside is much deeper than is often supposed. It is not so much that other people will think you are "funny," ~~though~~ this is a common and rationalized subsidiary incentive, but because you will feel more lonely by being different.

One of the curses of more theologically minded ages was the feeling of sure damnation which was liable to afflict sensitive people. When everyone else seemed to be taking part happily in church life, with assurance that all would be well, the inability to share in what was then the main group activity might bring conviction of incorrigible wickedness. The natural solitary was liable to see himself as Cain, either glorying unhappily in it like Byron or sinking into utter despair. Bunyan and Cowper, to mention only two noble creative minds, passed through this suffering. Readers may remember the wanderer met by George Borrow in *Lavengro* who was certain that he had somehow committed the sin against the Holy Ghost and could never be forgiven. Today the one who wishes to be a little apart, or is compelled to be so, thinks rather of being "unsociable," "not popular," "can't make friends." Many people of all ages, perhaps mostly the young, suffer a great deal from the fact that they do not particularly want to take part in all the things that other people do, and think that this must be a fault in themselves. The very existence of these activities seems to create the loneliness which in fact it only illuminates.

The situation in fact is one which needs a special kind of courage. Resistance to group activities may come from many reasons. There is the natural solitary who really prefers being alone with his thoughts to the continual and noisy company of others. There is the proud worker who wants nothing from the boss but a fair wage for his labor, who is suspicious of any attempt to give him more. There are those who believe that nothing is done without a purpose and that to accept a gift is to fall immediately into debt of one kind or another. They all need courage, and the greatest courage is not always shown in resistance.

There is nothing to be said for staying out of things simply because of the heroic feeling it gives you. Too many people are inclined to cherish their sufferings, and to add a few self-inflicted ones if the normal supply is not enough. Children who stay away from a longed-for party because they have quarreled with the little host are to be found behaving in the same way thirty or forty years later. Suffering has no merit in itself, only in its cause and the way in which it is accepted and directed. People who are very scornful of any idea of physical mortification for the good of the soul may heap a great deal of emotional mortification on themselves. They will not fast for love of God, but they will abstain from a wedding cake for the hate of men. So there is nothing good whatever in not going to the office party because of the way the boss spoke to you in the morning, or coming home early from the outing because you thought the manager's wife was too patronizing. Stay away if you like, but never think that you are doing anything noble.

When no principle is at stake, it may sometimes be right to suffer mildly for the greater pleasure of others. It is a pleasant thing to remember how you made those wretched youths turn off their portable radio; more pleasant perhaps to remember how you let them go on playing it. Your friends may be the poorer for your absence; they really do like to have you with them, queer, unsociable creature though you think yourself to be. There are better ways of serving people than by joining in their trivial pleasures; but this, too, is a kind of service, while sitting self-consciously alone is none. It may be satisfying to come away early because you feel insulted, but is it so satisfying for your husband to have to leave his beer and the children their games at the same time? The enjoyment that most people genuinely find in these many activities is good and not to be despised or diminished. A man who resists his shaping environment all the time must be sure of what he is doing. If the environment is bad, he has the duty of a prophet to denounce it by whatever means he can. Yet not all that is displeasing to one person is bad. There is a danger of becoming self-righteous and proud in judgment when standing apart is glorified in itself. He who was called the Son of Man came eating and drinking, leading the fullest life that his time and place offered; there were some who condemned him for it. Christians try to know, like their Master, when to withdraw into a quiet place and when to be with others at their pleasure.

The courage which is needed here is to accept the fact that group activities do not touch the real question of loneliness. The sense of belonging which they give will disappear as soon as there is no longer any external organization to hold the group together. The big firm will not extend its benevolence to those whom it no longer employs—and, in the terms of this world alone, why should it? Death or long illness makes the worker useless, and therefore ineligible for welfare and recreation that may once have increased his usefulness. A move to a different district tears you away from those you have come to call your friends. If there is true friendship, it survives the loss of physical presence; but it is an acid test of friendship nevertheless. If loneliness seems to be increased by a different environment, the true loneliness has never been faced. And although conditions of employment and security are probably better today than they have ever been before, they are not made certain for ever. Even today a depression, by whatever trade-marked name the economists may care to describe it, could mean the loss of employment and all that goes with it. The disaster of war would sweep away canteens and dance halls equally with armament factories; modern man is as naked and vulnerable before the unseen enemy as the cave man before the saber-toothed tiger. War would end all belonging and all caring in this world: which we all know, but sometimes regard as not polite to mention.

Can we therefore, cuddled and cherished as we are, yet horribly alone in the fear of annihilation, keep any integrity? "Pure religion and undefiled before God and the Father is this: to visit the fatherless and widows in their affliction, and to keep himself unspotted from the world." Can it be done? Christians are often accused of contracting out of the world, taking part in nothing, while they cherish their own progress to salvation. No aspect of Christian life has been so criticized, all through the centuries, as that of the enclosed religious orders. Yet the commandment is plain, and there are many others besides this particular verse. We are to do all we can to relieve suffering and promote joy; therefore there is good in the playing field and the factory clinic. Yet we are not to be so involved in them that we regard them as the only good. To take part in life as fully as possible, yet in such a way that you could bear the loss of any activity: that is the way of the Christian in the world. Even the good things can spot and defile, if they are made essential. Our dependence should be on nothing that man has made, though we may receive and honor man's work because man was made by God. Not long ago, men had to strive, often to suffer, that they might keep their integrity in the face of indifference, hostility and injustice from their employers. Now they more often have to keep integrity in the face of overwhelming benevolence. It is the "rapacious benevolence" of which Dickens wrote.

Now, criticism of existing trends is all very well. The intention behind it is not to produce a grim picture of the big firm and its manifold activities, or to discourage enjoying oneself with a group. If certain false images are being created, it is necessary to knock them down. Yet is the image false in every respect? There is undoubtedly a great deal of genuine affection and loyalty among workers in the same place, and even sometimes toward the firm itself. They are not all hypocrites on the seaside outing, but simply people enjoying themselves for the day with those who share common interests and depend on the same kind of work. Partly through the work of the firms themselves, and partly through the natural comradeship of the workers, the place of work often stands for more than a means of earning money. It may stand for more than the place where people live. Though it is not so in small country places, and less so in certain areas of industrial towns, the primary loyalty today is often directed away from the neighborhood where the home happens to be. The situation is most marked in the vast suburbs of London, where for many people home means just the one house where the immediate family lives. For many, especially if they are recent arrivals, there is practically no exchange of visits and hospitality in the district; sometimes there is literally no communication. Visitors come in their cars or by train from another district where the real contact may have been made. Suburban dwellers often know far more about those who work in the same office than about those who live next door.

For a very long time the Christian church, in all its branches, has been organized on a parochial system. People were expected to worship at the church or chapel within whose ambit their dwelling place lay. Since Sunday is the principal day of Christian worship and is also a day off work for most people, the parish church or local chapel must remain. But it is no use pretending that the primary loyalty always coincides with the parish boundaries. It did so when few people moved beyond those boundaries from birth to death, when dwellers only a few miles away were looked on as foreigners. If religion is to mean anything, it has to be carried into every aspect of the individual life; and attachment to the parish church alone can intensify the regrettable tendency, noted and rightly attacked by many critics, to bring out faith with the best suit on Sunday morning and put it back in the wardrobe for the rest of the week. The churches have recognized this and have done a great deal by the provision of special chaplains to factories, schools and universities. In London, the "guild churches" of the city provide plenty of weekday services for office workers, with the chance to hear some good midday sermons; the same type of thing is being done by all denominations in other parts of London. Many dioceses in industrial areas have an industrial missioner who is specially charged with the care of factory workers. The experiment of the "house church" which started at Halton in Yorkshire has spread, and it is not such a startling thing now for the Eucharist to be celebrated in a house or at the place of work. Yet there is a great deal more to be done. Because of the shortage of clergy, the appointment of a special chaplain often means that an overworked parish priest or local minister takes on a new additional responsibility. Since clergymen are subject to normal vices, the full-time chaplain sometimes gets into difficulties with the local man who claims a primary responsibility. But with all the failures and doubts and halting steps, the pastoral care of Christians is taking some new and exciting directions.

Here is a challenge to the lay Christian, and to all who profess a regard for Christian values. Some will cling to the parish system in its traditional form, sincerely believing it to be a failure of nerve and even of duty to adopt any other. Though life may not center on the group of dwellings, they argue, though it may be dull and difficult to worship with people who do not share your interests, surely this is no reason for changing it. Christianity was not meant to be easy. Indeed it was not; but while the Christian must not shrink from difficulties, we need not augment them. The road is usually stony enough without piling any extra rocks on it. If the parish system were clearly ordained by God, or if it had been used by the church from apostolic times, no change of circumstances should turn us from it. But it was in fact a comparatively late innovation, after Christianity had been generally accepted in the decaying Roman Empire, whose modes of organization it was often convenient to follow. This was for Christianity a part of the social pattern. We live in an age when it is not taken for granted: the "house church" is much closer to the similar conditions of the earliest Christian period.

Priests and other ministers do not make up the whole church. In the factory, in the office, on either side of the counter, in the classroom and the laboratory, there are opportunities to be taken. Here are common interests, some of which touch people in the deepest ways. More deeply perhaps than could be found among many "neighbors" in the modern sense of the word. The girl next door may be very charming, but the young man is likely to be more interested in the girl at the office whom he sees much more often. The songs round the drawing room piano were pleasant fifty years ago: the songs round the pub piano or in the returning coach may now draw people into a truer intimacy. A sense of belonging will always be false while it springs from mere juxtaposition. The real belonging comes from recognizing the individual, his faults, his needs and his essential loneliness. Love can truly be expressed by the provision of canteens, clubs and outings, if only these things are given for love of the people themselves, not for the temporary labels they are wearing. We have not yet some to terms with real loneliness, but we have advanced from the falsities of the gambler's "membership card." There are true loyalties in existence. Whether the objects of loyalty are always worthy is not to the point. From a common loyalty there can grow a common love. The casually linked arms may soon be parted; but they can also break the dark silence of ancient wrongs.

5

GETTING BETTER AND BETTER

"This here progress, it keeps going on," said Mr. Smallways at the beginning of the present century.[1] The event
which wrung from him this exclamation of mingled
wonder and anxiety was the building of a great mono-
rail from London to the coast. A foot of one of the
supporting pylons intruded on his back garden. With
true resourcefulness he used it, and the advertisement
panel attached to it, as a basis for his tool-shed. And
there, under the overshadowing image of twentieth-
century technology, Mr. Smallways pottered away happily while the powers of the world prepared to annihilate
each other. H. G. Wells caught the true voice of the
ordinary man, when he caused the word "progress" to
be applied to a new scientific discovery which could
be given practical effect. It is the advance of science
which comes to most people's minds when they say that
we have progressed in the last hundred years.

The outward signs of this advance are part of our daily
environment, unnoticed until they fail; a strike on public

[1] H. G. Wells, *The War in the Air*.

transport can still make human feet the quickest method
of getting from one place to another in a modern city.
There are few parts of the world which have not at
least some acquaintance with inventions which would
have reduced the most sophisticated European of a
hundred years ago to a state of gibbering wonder. Men
move through the air faster than sound, while sound itself
can be electrically transmitted at the speed of light.
Sound and sight can be recorded, stored, broken up and
reassembled many miles away, also mutilated, edited and
falsified. In 1789, a country parson wrote laconically
and comfortably in his diary: "Very great rebellion in
France, according to the papers," some two weeks after
the fall of the Bastille.[2] Today a revolution on the other
side of the world may be heard of in our homes within
minutes and seen in them within hours. We have seen
pictures of that which no human being ever saw from
the beginning of creation: the other side of the moon.
Men in orbit have literally fulfilled Puck's boast and "put
a girdle round about the earth in forty minutes." We
have killed tens of thousands in a single explosion and
speak familiarly of the ability to do the same in millions.
We are also able to cure diseases that were almost always
fatal fifty years ago and to restore bodies that seem to
be hopelessly shattered. In fact, it goes on and on.

Are we justified in believing that the whole human
situation has changed with equal speed? It is a question
to be considered, for it may appear that this belief under-
lies many of our problems. Judgment, and the actions

---

[2] James Woodforde, *Diary*, entry for July 24, 1789.

that follow it, may be wrongly influenced if we persist in regarding the age in which we live from the point of view of its differences from the past. The idea of progress, and the unreasoned optimism that it engenders, can force people into a stream of activities that tend far away from universal improvement. False pressures are strengthened by the fact that "modern" can be readily equated with "better."

The doctrine of general improvement makes an interesting social, political and literary study. Although it has long been linked with the cult of science and technology, and consequently has taken a few hard knocks from some of the more unsavory manifestations of that cult, it has a vigorous life of its own. The philosophy of history that is most widely held among those who are not professional historians is that movement in time is movement toward better things. An American commentator remarks of recent university graduates in his country: "The present, more than the past, is their model; while they share the characteristic American faith in the future also, they see it as more of the same." [3] A few years ago, a great classical humanist in England declared that he held the faith in progress as "a truth that lies somewhere near the roots of our religion." [4] The advertiser who tells us that his product is the "modern method for modern people" may be less nobly motivated, but he is sure of the same general response.

[3] Whyte, *op. cit.*, p. 73.

[4] Gilbert Murray, "Religio Grammatici" in *Essays and Addresses* (1921).

The idea of what man can and will achieve goes back to the Renaissance, with its roots thrust much deeper. When Marlowe wrote to be declaimed on the stage:

> Nature that framed us of four elements,
> Warring within our breasts for regiment,
> Doth teach us all to have aspiring minds,[5]

he was using a belief of medieval science to declare a faith that was only to grow in strength as the newer science displaced the old. John Donne might have more doubts about where "this here progress" was going to lead:

> And new philosophy calls all in doubt,
> The element of fire is put quite out,
> The sun is lost, and th' earth, and no man's wit
> Can well direct him where to look for it.[6]

but he went along with it and made poetry out of it all the same. The Royal Society was founded in 1662; the same spirit of inquiry which made Charles II and his cousin Rupert concoct experiments that sometimes went wrong, also impelled Newton to greater discoveries. A hundred years or more later, when "enthusiasm" ceased to be the term of reprobation that it had been for so long, radical notions of what mankind could do when tyranny was overthrown took shape in the doctrine of "perfectibility." Once more, there were to be no heights that man could not attain; Prometheus had been bound too long, and Faust was well on the way to canonization. And although the church tended now to be playing

[5] Christopher Marlowe, *Tamburlaine*, Part I, Act II. vii. 18-20.
[6] John Donne, "The First Anniversary."

the part of devil's advocate against these newly proposed saints, Science and Perfectibility continued to trot amiably hand-in-hand. New discoveries in zoology and geology challenged the letter of the Bible, causing many catastrophes of faith for reasons which now seem ludicrous to Christian and agnostic alike, but which seemed tragically sufficient at the time. There were some to deplore the prevailing optimism, and look wistfully toward a glorious past in an idealized Athens or a romantic Middle Ages; these too did their share of harm, and we must look at them later. But the general view was that everything was not only getting better but must inevitably do so.

The belief that development in time is always from the less good to the better outlives in popular estimation its demise in the minds of more profound thinkers. Edmund Wilson has pointed out how T. S. Eliot drew from Flaubert and Laforgue some of his impatience with the sterile and degenerating present.[7] Socialists like Morris and Wells believed that human arrogance and injustice, bolstered by ever-increasing technical power, would lead to upheaval and mass destruction before the old radical dream of the Golden Future could be realized; and Morris indeed threw many a backward glance to what he fondly believed to have been Merrie England, a byroad which later enticed the crusading feet of Belloc and the tremendously humane sanity of Chesterton. Huxley and Orwell saw coming disaster, without any hope of climbing back. But for

[7] Edmund Wilson, *Axel's Castle* (New York: 1953), p. 100.

the greater number of people, the modern creed is simpler
and more comforting. If something new and more tech-
nically difficult is possible, it ought to be done. The
presence in the world of a new skill, a new "know-how,"
is a sign of progress. There can be no question that
technical discoveries and inventions have improved the
lot of mankind as well as imperiling its survival. But
there is too much tendency today to welcome a thing
uncritically because it is new and more complicated or
requires greater skill to produce. A member of one
of the record clubs unwittingly spoke up for his generation when the first rumors were heard of records revolv-
ing at 16 2/3 revolutions per minute. "If these are the
latest thing," he wrote to the "club magazine," "then
let's have them—I'm all for progress." I, too, am all for
improvements in recorded sound; but there did seem
here to be uncritical equation of the "latest thing" with
"progress," a supposition that spreads far beyond this
trivial example. The new invention must be installed
and used everywhere, without regard to its goodness or
whether it is appropriate. A very large new hotel had
hardly risen from its foundations when a board dis-
played on its supporting girders announced that every
bedroom would have "bath, radio, television and stereophonic sound." The desire for stereophonic sound in
a place that should be designed rather for silence suggests
a Gadarene urge to put into full effect everything that
has become practicable. The first water taps were not
fitted into every wall in the house, just to show how
progressive the owner was. We are not so far from the

Brave New World. Presumably the stereophonic sound is still under the control of the occupant, but just wait and see how long that freedom lasts. We already have compulsory and interminable piped music in some places of work.

Those who claim to believe in inevitable progress, and who couple it with the advance of science, must realize what they are really saying. They are making scientific newness a good in itself. They may refuse traditional values of good and evil, and may even deny that such values can be meaningfully expressed, but they are in fact introducing a strong sense of values into the whole tendency of the times. It is possible to look at the world around us, the world of factories and railways, transmitters and computers, and say that all this represents real progress. It is possible to look at it and say that it represents regress and degeneration. To do either of these things is to impose values on the observed facts, to find an essence in the various accidentals, to make a moral judgment. The point would not need to be brought out if it were not for the double-think of people who say that they don't care about old-fashioned ideas of good and evil, because the world is getting better without such notions. It is, of course, also possible to take a third view and say that computers and so on are morally neutral: they are existing and observed phenomena, and there are values by which their use can be adjudged good or bad. This is what the Christian does say, unless the new idolatry has ensnared him or has driven him to an obscurantist flight from the realities of his present state. For we must see clearly the world in which we live, for we derive what we are partly by being here and now instead of somewhere else. The duty that does not change with new discoveries is the duty to keep looking closely and asking what effect everything is having on the whole life of man.

Each new invention, each technique that is brought to perfection by long and patient research, is immediately capable of causing men to act virtuously or to sin, to use the old-fashioned terms that are by no means out of place yet. Human choice is still demanded, and is determined by factors and pressures that go far beyond the technical "know-how." The belief in progress which the perfectibility theorists brought into a world of rapidly increasing scientific growth was based on the axiom, scarcely ever then challenged, that an increase in factual knowledge and the use of reason would lead to an increase in the nobility and unselfishness of man. Progress of this kind needs elements which have been too often forgotten. The moral and spiritual side of man is neither inhibited by primitive physical conditions nor outmoded by complex ones. The potentialities for good or bad actions are always there. Some conditions may make the exercise of virtue easier or harder; but this world is the place for us to live our bodily life, and what we make of it is no passing accident. This vast technical civilization is a product of the same free will which enables us to make what use we like of our own creatures. Perhaps instead of saying that the computer is morally neutral, we had better say that it is morally ambivalent.

Yet it is clear that material well-being can normally be described as "better" than material poverty, disease and want. It is as well to pause over this and not be led into a high-sounding moral condemnation of science and all it has done for humanity. Christians have often been charged with an excess of other-worldliness, fixing their eyes on the heavenly City while neglecting the earthly city. Indeed the contrast between the two types of city has for a very long time been painful, not to say ironical. There is a good deal of truth in these accusations. Not only have individual Christians neglected their duties to their neighbors, in plain disregard of the injunctions of the gospel, but whole Christian groups have been found indifferent to suffering. Christianity has tended to sway between an extreme individual piety and a narrow obsession with social work which has diminished spiritual power. There can be no doubt after the most cursory reading of the New Testament that the right course lies in the middle, neglecting neither aspect. The Apostles were powerful in preaching, efficient in their relief work in times of famine and distress. The Christian is bound to do all he can to relieve suffering and improve physical conditions. This is an absolute duty and the very letter of Christ's teaching lays it upon him. The spirit of that teaching takes it further. We cannot go on relieving poverty and suffering by means that were available two hundred, fifty, even twenty years ago. If science has provided better means, it is a sin not to use them for good. King Wenceslaus could be called "good" for a gift of pine logs; this does not mean that our aged poor must choke over a wood fire now that we have discovered central heating. The Samaritan bathed the traveler's wounds with oil and wine and set him on his own beast; but we should fail in our duty to the suffering children of Africa and Asia if we did not give them penicillin and fly them to a hospital. We have no right to speak a single word against the misuse of science unless we are prepared to make the fullest use of what science has given us for good. There can be talk of "progress" if we emulate the Good Samaritan with the more efficient means which are now at our disposal. The word becomes more than inappropriate if our new inventions carry us along so fast that we cannot see who is lying at the side of the road.

The only standard by which to judge material changes and increasing technical complexity is the way in which they affect the individual. Every act of compassion is valid for what it does to relieve individual suffering. The opportunities fall in our way, and sometimes we are looking too far into space to see them. If Christians have been rightly accused of looking for rewards in a heaven located somewhere in the sky, modern man may be said to be reaching out for the moon before they have learned to walk in justice and mercy on the earth. The frenzied and jealous attempts of the great nations to get out to our satellite instead of making this world safe, would seem to be lunatic in every sense of the word. Service is to the individual, as we meet him in church, at the street corner, in the prison cell—or even in the space rocket, if that should come to pass. To do good wherever the opportunity arises is the Christian duty. It is the only way in which some beginning can be made in this world of anger and suspicion. Even the grubbier aspects of life may have their moments of truth. This is not to say that the Christian must shun the big relief organization. To insist on being Lady Bountiful carrying a basket of food around the village may be a sinful waste when the same amount of time and money could feed a whole district by modern methods. The man who crawls out of the shelter to give what aid he can when bombs are falling is a hero; but if the aircraft are dropping food and medical supplies, he is a fool not to cooperate with them. The individual Sir Galahad would be a nuisance in the middle of a United Nations relief force. Yet we can dare to speak of progress only if every member of that force has his heart's desire set on the Holy Grail and sees its holiness in every individual whose suffering he may hope to ease in love.

Not only is our quest directed always to the individual, it goes on without any thought of whether relief is deserved. The Samaritan did not ask for references from the wounded traveler, and Christ healed many who needed the forgiveness of sins which he also gave them. The charity which demands a guarantee of respectability is "charity" in the coldest and most degrading sense that the word came to have during the nineteenth century: it has nothing to do with the *agape* or perfect love of the New Testament. True charity is an all or nothing operation. And here, indeed, the modern secular relief organizations may show more nobly than many Christian groups. The large scale on which help to distressed areas is organized gives no time for a separation of the population into the deserving and the undeserving. "I'm one of the undeserving poor," says Shaw's dustman, cheerfully and proudly, at a time when a ticket for soup in the name of Christ was given to those who would submit to a long and often humiliating interrogation about their attendance at church and sending the children to Sunday school. Yes, there are signs of "this here progress"; we have come to recognize the absolute right of the individual to be properly clothed and sheltered, warmed and fed. This is simply what Christ taught, but it has taken nearly two thousand years to get round to it. Now that we are all full of good will, our leaders might make two important corrections in their thinking. First, they might stop acting in a way that makes it seem ominously possible that every individual will be blown to pieces in the new FHA-financed home and all. Also, they might stop thinking, or appearing to think, that the provision of material welfare is going to make the slightest difference to individual conduct. The modern state does not demand a certificate of goodness before giving benefits. But the naïve belief in inevitable progress is still there, expecting that the outwardly clean will become inwardly clean too. It seems a strange paradox that socialists, who for so long condemned the rich as utterly wicked, believe that the giving of comparative riches to the poor will make them utterly good. It is not such a simple equation. There was great heroism and sacrifice to be found sometimes in the concentration camps: there

can be lust in nylon sheets and envy over the smartest
new television set.

Unless we are prepared to employ all our resources
for individual betterment, without demanding either
previous good conduct or subsequent reformation, we
are holding a strange idea of progress. What can all this
change lead to but a continual drifting, as life becomes
materially more easy and at the same time more complicated? Is the choice between annihilation by powers
that we cannot control, or submergence in perpetual,
boring idleness? The world of 1984, torn by war and
cruelty, is terrible. The worlds of the great future
promised by thinkers like Morris and Shaw are rather
depressing. When Morris has brought us to the end of
News from Nowhere, we have heard of so many things
which have been abolished that we are not clear what
is positively left to do. The hygienic world of the
Ancients that closes the cycle of five plays, *Back to
Methuselah*, seems dull and desiccated after the plays
about unregenerate existing society, even if we could
be sure that all its inhabitants could talk as wittily as
Shaw makes them. Shaw recognized this dilemma without solving it, and ends with the recognition in the
Epilogue:

> For what may be beyond, the eyesight of Lilith is too
> short; it is enough that there is a beyond.

The fact is, of course, that there will always be conflict,
because of the very uniqueness and loneliness of each
individual. The dilemma of utopia is brought about by

the supposition that material changes in environment will make a noticeable difference to the natures of human beings. There will always be things to strive for, always the desire to love and protect and the misery of having that desire frustrated. Yet it is so commonly held as a matter of faith that people are changing as the world around them changes, that the belief in inevitable progress has brought its own judgment. The fear of being different grows stronger, as the opportunities for material comforts and pleasures become greater. There is often a frenzied pursuit of the latest inventions, the novelties which an affluent society assures us are making life more enjoyable. When from newspapers, hoardings and television screens we are told that everything is getting better, the sense that all is not well has to be suppressed as a shameful disease. In this world of gleaming kitchens and happy housewives, clean young lovers made immortal not on a Grecian urn but on a colored advertisement for cigarettes, anyone who admits to being lonely seems to be deliberately cutting himself off from a benevolent society. There is the evil of the belief in progress equated with scientific development, as it appears in popular form at the present time. It creates a false security which is no security, invites escape which is no refuge. Men are, as ever, fearful, guilty, naked; also brave, noble and redeemed. But they are not allowed to see their true selves. Once again, there comes the fear of the "terrible It."

So we may be "all for progress" and yet stand amazed and doubtful in the complexity which passes for it. That there is loss and gain in human affairs as the years pass, both for the individual and for the whole race, seems to be a proposition beyond denial. Progress or regress must depend on which way the balance tips when both are weighed at any given time. Historians, sociologists and specialists of all kinds may have their answers when they look at the events of the last hundred and fifty years. But for each individual, interesting though the answer may be, it has no binding force. For each individual, the present time is reality, and present time is measured not only by the ticking of a clock but by the whole complexity which makes him what he is. He is a creature of his age and his environment, and many thinkers have understood this, only to lie down and say that individual striving is of no avail. But precisely the opposite is true. All that the individual does is done within his environment and has some effect, however tiny, on that environment. Society does not grow up by chance but by the wills of countless individual people. He who finds himself submerged in society creates his submergence by that very realization. This is our place, this here and now. To be born in the Periclean Age of Greece might have been very fine, but it was not so for us. To have avoided the worst times of the Industrial Revolution is good, but it does not guarantee us perfect happiness today. We stand in a total situation, which includes our awareness of the past and our ability to make judgments about it. Progress is the result not of inventions but of the use which men make of them. Here, as in all things, choice is demanded of every individual. To live in a highly scientific age is neither reward nor punishment: it is that which *is*. The challenge comes to each one in his loneliness, as it always has.

6

OR WORSE AND WORSE

THE BELIEF in inevitable progress did not go unchallenged during the nineteenth century. There were many who, true to the human tendency towards personal and universal nostalgia, looked coldly on the march of science and the overthrow of kings, and proclaimed only woe to the inhabitants of the earth. In Peacock's satirical novel *Headlong Hall* (1816) we meet Mr. Foster the optimist, who believes that the new age of enlightenment has dawned and is growing ever brighter, and Mr. Escot the pessimist, who sees only degeneration and ruin with every passing moment. We have let Mr. Foster have his say. His opponent is equally vocal and perhaps equally out of balance. While most people today hold, in some way or other, that the world is getting better and life is easier, the contrary opinion has had its effect on art and literature, and on popular opinion as well. Many people find no difficulty in holding the two contradictory views simultaneously and keeping them apart. Old men who will say in one breath that life is happier and better than when they were young, will add in the next breath that society and its standards have

sadly deteriorated. Which is right? It is time to give
a hearing to Mr. Escot.

To see a general decline is, indeed, much older than
Peacock's character. It is probable that at some time a
primitive man deplored the new degenerate habit of
cooking meat instead of eating it raw from the kill.
Certainly for as long as men have expressed themselves
in any form of written record, the backward-looking
faculty has been strongly exercised. It is a belief common to many cultures that there was a Golden Age,
long ago in the past, when all was fair and lovely, when
there was no war, when corn grew without sowing and
the vine bowed down with fruit of its own accord.
The Golden Age faded away, and mankind passed
through the ages of silver and bronze to the present one
of lead, in which life is hard and grim. Jews and Christians spoke of the Garden of Eden from which man had
been expelled for his rebellion of will; and that image
of the garden as the perfect world, safe, enclosed and
identified with the innocence of childhood, recurs often
in many forms of art. The Elizabethans were impressed,
almost obsessed, by the idea of mutability. The world
was running down; its divinely-ordered hierarchy was
dissolving back into the chaos out of which all had been
created. One of the great divisions in human thought
came about at the time of the French Revolution, when
men like Godwin spoke of "perfectibility" and looked
not back but forward to the Golden Age. But where
the optimist saw strength and promise in the new society,
Blake saw only the "dark, Satanic mills."

Today there are many who follow Blake and Mr. Escot in decrying urban life, industry, science, technology. They show that the shining medal of inevitable progress has a darker reverse side. Looking for an escape, they find the Golden Age in the past but believe that it can be restored. The answer must be "back to nature." Man has indeed lost his primal innocence, but he can find it again. Life in towns of his own making, dark, dirty and overcrowded, has killed his joy and stifled his natural love of life. If he would be a free spirit again, he must find and follow what was true in man before civilization degraded him. The proponents of this belief range from kindly people who weave their own tweed suits and claim to keep very fit by eating nuts, to the more aggressive writers like Lawrence and the Powys brothers. Shaw himself, believing in man's great future, believed also that many of the forms and conventions of modern society must be cast aside if our race was not to be superseded like the dinosaurs. He called for conscious cooperation with the Life Force, the deliberate selection that would breed the Superman: a kind of vegetarian and rationalist Siegfried.

On a more popular level, we have had a generation or more of songs that glorify country life. The man who is a wage slave in the city may assert himself in the country: whether over the local inhabitants or the sheep is not made clear. A long walk in the country is extolled as a cure for everything. Few seem to take this cheap therapy today, but perhaps sitting in a closed car on a country road is thought to be a contribution toward it. Certainly the urge toward camping holidays is as strong as ever. The true camp, private and in a tent, attracts many; but also the most crowded type of holiday, heavy with all the paraphernalia of modern scientific civilization, goes by the name of holiday camp. Established in the United States and pressing hard in Britain, is the attempt to find a new market for modern devices by associating them with the open air and the "natural life." When the kitchen is too crowded with shining equipment, it may be fun to have a barbecue in the garden; but the barbecue is now likely to incorporate an electric roaster, linked by a cable with the reassuring power of the kitchen itself. Clothing of a type that was once made for the rough country worker and therefore despised in the city is now sold at a high price as the smartest thing for weekends. Then there are the desert island fantasies which provide many ideas for comic strips and keep a program on the BBC in weekly business. It is worth looking further at the origins and development of all this, for it reflects some of the deepest fears and tensions in modern man.

When modern philosophers began to examine the nature of the state which had evolved from social and religious catastrophes, the move toward theories of perfectibility began as well. If the new forms of government were worth preserving—and writers were anxious for many reasons to prove that they were—mankind could not have deteriorated continually from the past Golden Age. Hobbes looked with horror on the "state of nature," in which each man sought only to preserve his own life and to dominate that of others. Continual struggles made life "nasty, brutish and short"; there was neither justice nor injustice, for the absence of any fixed reference meant that there was nothing but war. At the same time, Milton shuddered at the idea of all savage and disordered things. The dreadful wood in *Comus*, through which the two brothers seek their sister who is entrapped by the wild, "natural" rout, is the primal Garden gone wrong. Locke was vague about what he understood by the "state of nature," though he made some side comments on what Hobbes understood by it. He seemed convinced that the rule of reason somehow prevailed in it.

It was not long before a different view began to be heard. Men were traveling more widely; news of other civilizations was breaking through. The great questions of the day—liberty, justice, ownership of property and so on—were found to exist and even to be answered in remote parts of the world. What was more, scholarship was proving that they had been discussed in civilizations that had long disappeared. It really looked as if a serious approach to those problems did not depend on an enlightened society supported by Christian ethics. Was there not something inherent in mankind which impelled him toward the good? If the virtuous pagans of antiquity could be favorably compared with certain later tendencies, did it not follow that even more primitive peoples would show more of the essential good? So the brutish inhabitants of Hobbes' state of nature gave way to the notion of the "noble savage." [1] It was civilization and the town which had corrupted mankind. If he could live in his primitive state, he would be wholly good and pure. The Golden Age might still exist in places where the dirty hand of society had not reached. When Defoe wrote *Robinson Crusoe*, he never imagined that he was inspiring many future adventure books for boys, still less many Christmas pantomimes. Crusoe, alone on his desert island, at first regards his isolation as hateful, perhaps a punishment for his past sins. But after many years of solitude he finds his true self, and his true relationship with God. The savage whom he names Man Friday is a splendid creature— loving, honest and loyal, because he has never been ensnared by civilization. It was not for its literary merits alone that *Robinson Crusoe* was so popular, in spite of plenty of evidence that men shipwrecked or marooned on desert islands were more likely to revert to animalism.

The idea of the "splendid savage" found a congenial companion in an older tradition. Just as faith in perfectibility was to join forces with faith in scientific progress, so the splendid savage was not too far out of place in the pastoral convention. This, too, had its origins in antiquity and had been revived soon after the Renaissance. Medieval nature-poetry is truly natural. It is not mannered or self-conscious, but expresses the true feeling of people who lived close to the earth and its changing seasons. For the countryside was never

[1] See, e.g., Bertrand Russell, *History of Western Philosophy* (London: 1946), pp. 714 f., 720.

far away, even in the towns, and conditions were not very different for the burgher and the peasant. It needed the growth of towns like London and Paris to great cities, and the comparative stability of the court after its years of continual wandering, to produce an artificial longing for simple country life. The Elizabethans handled it elegantly, but held firmly to what slight comforts and technical devices their civilization could offer. To hunt in the countryside was one thing, but to live in a cottage and work in the fields was quite another. In most of the pastoral plays and poems of the time, it is assumed that the prince who disguises himself for a time as a shepherd will have with him all the food, clothing and servants that he wishes. Shakespeare, who often shows himself to be above his contemporaries in basic common sense as well as genius, wrote one of the loveliest pastoral comedies, but satirized the convention at the same time. The Duke in *As You Like It* who says when he is in exile:

> Hath not old custom made this life more sweet
> Than that of painted pomp?

has no hesitation about returning when he is restored to his dukedom, leaving only the melancholy Jacques to nurse his honest renunciation in the "abandoned cave." The ambivalent feelings of the courtier toward the countryside are summed up by Touchstone:

> Truly, shepherd, in respect of itself, it is a good life; but in respect that it is a shepherd's life, it is naught. In respect that it is solitary, I like it very well; but in respect that it is private, it is a very vile life. Now in respect that it is

in the fields, it pleaseth me well; but in respect it is not in the court, it is tedious. As it is a spare life, look you, it fits my humour well; but as there is no more plenty in it, it goes much against my stomach.

Yet the pastoral convention endured. Marie Antoinette and her ladies were playing at shepherdesses almost to the eve of the French Revolution. Classical tradition, as well as biblical imagery of the sheep and the Good Shepherd, combined with growing unease in the towns which had become overgrown and consequently corrupt in every sense of the word.[2] Yet while the shepherd's life was idealized, it was possible also to sneer at simple country manners and ignorance. The word "urbane" is only a variant of "urban," yet it comes to stand for what is polished and elegant. The word "boor" originally means "farmer"; a "clown" is a countryman. But while these tensions were building up, and the rural scene was at the same time despised and desired, the cult of primitivism was taking a more positive turn.

In France, while the court ladies were sitting around with ornamental crooks and Watteau was painting them doing it, somebody was trying to live the simple life in his own way. Rousseau got so far as selling his watch because he would live by the sun and never need to tell the time, but he did not go very far in his personal imitation of the "splendid savage." He did, however, write with biting wit, and indeed with what can only be called urbanity, about his beliefs. Man

[2] Hallett Smith, *Elizabethan Poetry* (Harvard: 1952), pp. 2 ff.

is naturally good, but is made bad by all the institutions which compose modern civilized life. The Romantics seized on this belief; disliking the institutions within which they found themselves forced to live, they were ready to have them swept away for the sake of true, unspoiled human nature. Things might, indeed, be getting better and better, but only because man was rediscovering his real self that had been forgotten and overlaid for so long. There was at first no conflict between primitivism and progress. The poets glorified the emotions and sensations; even the gentle Keats called for "a life of emotions rather than thoughts." The ideal was to be found nearer home than Robinson Crusoe's island. The peasant had a nobler part than the pastoral convention had yet granted him. Living closer to nature, he was thus closer to the mystic impulses of earth and air by which men should live. Wordsworth strode through the countryside, a gaunt figure who must have sorely tried the patience of leech-gatherers and others if his reported encounters with them are even half true. It was his belief that:

> One impulse from a vernal wood
>   May teach you more of man,
> Of moral evil and of good,
>   Than all the sages can.

In Britain the Romantic movement is kindly thought of, associated as it is with some of Britain's finest poetry. We think of daffodils and nightingales, a gentle interest in the supernatural and a colorful touch of medievalism. But Germans who are liberally minded are apt to bare their teeth at the word "Romanticism." The cult of all that was primitive gave strength to the revival of ancient Germanic legends in which National Socialism found many of its perverted ideals. The German Youth Movement, antedating Hitler in its first revolt against existing standards, was essentially Romantic in its emotional and irrational approach to current conditions. There were the seeds of good and of evil in it, but it was the evil which burgeoned into the screaming masses at Nuremberg, the slaughter of millions of human beings like cattle, the nemesis which swept full circle to Nuremberg again. Beginning with the cult of Life, to be lived freely and without artificial restraint, it ended in the cult of death and destruction. The founders of the *Wandervögel* ("wandering birds") followed the familiar pattern. They identified themselves with the peasants, slept and ate more roughly than the peasants themselves, and tried to show their toughness and endurance in every way. Old Germanic rituals were revived, special favor being given to those which tested courage and physical strength. Otto Zarek relates his initiation into the *Wandervögel*: how he and his companions leapt naked through a fire while old Germanic songs were chanted. That was in 1913.[3] While in Britain our folk heritage was being defended by a few self-conscious Morris dancers, Germany was preparing to devastate Europe.

It is hardly surprising, therefore, that many people took, and continue to take, a gloomier view of the savage.

[3] Otto Zarek, *German Odyssey*, pp. 37 ff.

Long even before the *Wandervögel,* there were many
who looked neither for inevitable progress nor for a
blissful return to unspoiled primitivism. The reaction
grew more pessimistic; and like all pessimism it ground
to a halt. Yet even if many fine writers and thinkers
were stuck gnashing their teeth in their own private
Slough of Despond, their warnings were timely and too
often unheeded. Since there are still many who blame
human loneliness and anxiety on the corrupting powers
of modern urban civilization, we cannot afford to ignore
those who have spoken on the other side. In the nineteenth century many people who found themselves
unable to give honest assent to the doctrines of Christianity yet regarded those doctrines as the last bulwark
against barbarism. The snarls of the savage were already
being heard in some countries; if his patrons continued
to believe in his innocence and to foster him in every
way, it would be not a Golden Age but a new Dark
Age that was to be unleashed upon the West. The
personal excesses of those who claimed to follow where
the first Romantics had led were by no means reassuring.[4]
Even Nietzsche, who was no friend to Christianity and
has in fact been made to bear some of the blame for
Hitlerism, was more than impatient of the theories which
were expressing themselves in myths of social purity
and the glorification of physical power. Though he
formulated some of these theories he was honest enough

[4] For a detailed examination of these trends, see Mario Praz, *The
Romantic Agony* (Oxford: 1933).

to realize their dangers when put into practice by those who were all "obedience and long legs."

All these forebodings proved to be justified to an extent far beyond expectations. The twentieth century soon made it clear that, beneath the thin veneer of civilization, there lurked no splendid savage in pristine innocence but a ravening beast. While some people were getting back to nature in tented camps in the fields, others were losing the very shape of men in concentration camps. By the time 1945 came and brought its revelations of horror which even the years of war had not reached, there could be little doubt of the real issue. When men lose all that millennia of growth have given them—shelter, clothes, regular food, freedom from sudden violence—they return not to Eden but to the lowest circle of hell. Hobbes may have been a bit shaky on his anthropology and prehistory, but he was not so far wrong after all. Whatever residue of nobility and courage may survive in a few, the majority deteriorate as the trappings of civilization slip away one by one.

Many writers have told us as much, before and after the war, if we would take notice of them. Joseph Conrad feared the beast that lurked under the semblance of man, the beast who was released by the storm and the disasters at sea. Nature is no friend to man, but tolerates him and even submits to him only for a time. The ancients were wise, who knew that Pan was no jolly Falstaffian god but a power who could tear men away from all they knew as reality, and make them mad. Aldous Huxley, after years of satirizing the follies of his age, and hinting that those follies barely concealed the most primitive passions, tore aside pretence and wrote his most terrifying book. *Ape and Essence* (1949) has scarcely even the grim humor of the earlier *Brave New World*. It tells of civilization destroyed by atomic warfare. The survivors live among the ruins, burning books to keep themselves warm and disinterring corpses to find clothes. Only the worst features of the twentieth century remain—bureaucracy and the rule of fear. In *Brave New World* the young man called the Savage had overtones of Rousseau, nobly defying the barbarous efficiency of triumphant science. But in *Ape and Essence* there is no nobility: even man's faculty of devotion is bent toward the Devil instead of God. In short, as the archvicar of the diabolical cult puts it:

There are no limits. Anyone is capable of anything—but anything.

"There are no limits": that seems to be the message, too, of William Golding, one of the most important English novelists of the present day. His books continually warn of the beast in man, crouching only just below the surface, ready to spring as soon as the artificial barrier is lowered. Mankind has progressed since before recorded history to the position which he now holds. But life in society is only a compromise, a concession to the fact that if men are not formally polite they will cut each other's throats instead. A gloomy view? Yes, and one which does not tell the whole story, since it

tends to judge progress only by the outward signs.
But the events of the last two generations give us little
reason to feel complacent about what our ancestors have
built up, since we seem capable of destroying their work
in much shorter time than it took to create. The conflict
between Neanderthal Man and *homo sapiens*, about
which Golding writes in *The Inheritors*, still wages in
each one of us. That tension, that awareness of being
as Yeats said "fastened to a dying animal," that knowledge of noble aspirations dragged down by bodily weakness, is part of what we call our loneliness. The desert
island has been considerably eroded since Robinson
Crusoe landed there, and the Swiss Family Robinson
and Ballantyne's young heroes lived lives of perfect
felicity and innocence. The boys in Ballantyne's books
kept up the best British tradition and emerged unscathed,
even ennobled, by their exile. How different is the
story which Golding tells in *Lord of the Flies*, when
an aircraft full of schoolboys comes down on a remote
island. At first they go on living as if they were still
at school, the older boys taking charge, making rules
and seeing that everything is done decently. But
gradually the trappings of civilization drop away. The
strongest lead, and the mob follows them. Prowess in
hunting replaces skill on the cricket field. Before long
they are full of nameless terrors, worshiping the totem
of a pig in an attempt to propitiate the evil which has
come upon them. They become naked, painted savages,
hunting with wooden spears those who go against the
will of the majority. Yet the arrival of a British naval

ship brings them back at once to shamefaced obedience. "Jolly good show. Like the Coral Island," says the uncomprehending naval officer who rescues them; but:

> In the middle of them, with filthy body, matted hair and unwiped nose, Ralph wept for the end of innocence, the darkness of man's heart.

Lord of the Flies is a powerful book, which reminds us that the Fall is repeated in every human life and the whole life of man in society. A similer theme is in *Pincher Martin.* A drowned sailor lives through his own private purgatory on a desolate rock in the Atlantic, seeing all his worthless past life in retrospect, now that he is alone and deprived of all which had gone to make the environment for that life. In *Free Fall* it is the isolation and terror of a prison camp which makes the protagonist see himself as he really is. Crusoe knew that God was with him even on the desert island. Pincher Martin, with more loss because he has lived in a more elaborate civilization, believes himself to be quite cut off from every level of communication. William Golding, it seems to me, has stated the answer to primitivism, has stated it boldly and with great artistic skill. Man is not made nobler by being exposed to the elements, brought nearer to nature. The "blue dome" beneath which some have claimed to come nearer to God seems more often to reflect human nakedness and dependence. The fact that we have slowly overcome the hazards of nature—though great catastrophes of flood and earthquake can still make our works appear very frail—does not mean that the lonely individual is any better equipped to face her challenge than his primeval ancestor. People can get harmless fun out of "back to naturism" only because their view is that of a society which seldom sees nature as she is. To hunt in a red coat after foxes, "the unspeakable in the pursuit of the uneatable," is different in kind as well as in degree from the primitive chase of the unspeaking after the eatable.

There is no refuge here. When the trappings of civilized society are torn away, it is not to reveal a forgotten paradise that will save us from the anxieties falsely engendered by urban life. The man who has lost all will find no splendid savage to take away his loneliness as Friday did for Crusoe. The man he does find may well seem to be a stranger, savage if far from splendid, for he will be brought face to face with himself. Loneliness in its essence will appear when all the daily palliatives of loneliness have gone; and this direct self-revelation is indeed an important element in Golding's books.

Take your tent if you like, and pitch it on the most desolate slopes that this crowded world can offer. Draw your water from the well—or from the running stream if you admit no compromise—light your campfire by rubbing two sticks together. There is no escape, for the anxieties that you had thought to leave were sitting firmly on the pack which you carried so proudly away from the great city. Those anxieties were expressed in images of machines, meaningless masses, abstruse cal-

culations. Did you think that they could not come
rushing in with another face out of the empty night?
The centuries of civilization may lie in a thin veneer
that can easily be cracked. It is good to be able to face
existence without that slight protection, if that particular kind of courage is demanded. But to throw it
off violently is no courage but an escape that once
more proves to be no escape. If you put your trust in
the primitive state of man, it cannot stop with washing
in cold water or not at all, and eating without forks.
It is to be cast back into dependence not on the wildest
moods of nature only, but on her lightest whims. It
is to be at the mercy of every disease, to fear every
animal that has claws and teeth, to look for nothing
but violence from those outside your immediate circle.
Modern business may fairly be described as a jungle,
but jungle methods are neither improved nor worsened
by changing from black coats to unsewn skins. What
remains constant is the nature of the beast: the beast
is man.

Is there no reconciliation then? Are we forced to
choose between blind faith in a golden future which
seems to be ever receding, or stubborn commitment to
a golden past which has left very little trace? Can there
possibly be a way out of the dilemma, other than a dull
acquiescence in each moment without trying to find any
way of judging its essential quality? There is a doctrine,
which has already peeped into these pages, which is
bold enough to give the great paradox that alone can
set us free. There was a golden past, in the sense that

man was created with the perfect goodness of God set within him, with a world that could yield nothing but good. How he fell, what act or series of acts, what dawning awareness of good and evil seduced him, is beyond conjecture and can probably never be better expressed than through the poetic imagery of the first chapters of Genesis. There is a golden future, for man is not to be always dragged down by the beast. Every individual holds with his loneliness and his shame, the possibility of returning forever to that perfection from which he fell. This is a great mystery, and even divine revelation cannot allow us to bear much of its light. Yet one thing is certain: the falling and the rising are through choice. The exercise of will by each individual goes on, whatever the environment may be. It is something worth thinking about, on those cold nights round the camp fire.

7

LOVE ONE ANOTHER

THERE IS an answer which every reader who has got thus far must be demanding to hear. Is not the problem of loneliness solved by the affection which one human being can feel for another; or which a group can feel commonly among all its members? Not to be bought for an annual subscription, deeper than the loyalty of the workplace or neighborhood, simple affection seems to be above all criticism. It is independent of the technical state of civilization, and cares little for philosophical reflections on whether or not the world is getting better. It can tame even the beast that is in man. Need we look any further?

We might look a great deal further without ever getting to the heart of the matter. Words like "affection," "liking," "friendship," "regard" and, most of all, "love," are used in so many different and sometimes contradictory ways and to describe so many complex arrangements of the emotions, that we can get into considerable difficulties of language simply in trying to agree what we mean.[1] The ordinary man will be impatient of such

[1] This question is admirably discussed in C. S. Lewis, *The Four Loves* (New York: Macmillan, 1960).

distinctions and will prefer to quote particular examples. Love is the feeling he has had for his parents for as long as he could remember; feels now for his wife and children; has felt, perhaps for a number of girls who are only dim memories in a bundle of faded letters; feels for a few of his friends, though nothing would drag the word out of him in that connection. Well, that covers a fair set of similar but not identical emotions for a start; so we will not embarrass him further by asking him whether he loves his country, or was heard to say last week that he loved apple pie and cream. What can we find that is common to the love of family and of friends of both sexes?

In the first place, it is free of all ideological bias. We may be drawn into the company of those who share our beliefs about how things are and how they ought to be, but mere intellectual agreement is not enough for affection. Most Christians would admit that their best friends are often believers in other religions or in none. in Britain at least, political opponents can get on very well together in private life. Disputes within families on matters of principle do not strike at the real affection which holds them together: if they do, something is lacking in that affection. A common interest, whether in international politics, fly-fishing or going to art exhibitions, is often the occasion of affection, but seldom its cause. Then this love is free from the demands of service and duty, though it fulfills these demands if it is real. A truly loving husband and wife do not stop loving each other because one of them has washed up more often; a pair of friends do not argue about who is going to pay for the next drink. The service of love has its special courtesy, by which each member vies with the other to give most, but there is no balance sheet to be duly audited.

Love does not even ask whether its object is worthy, but rather feels unworthiness in itself. In this way the ideal of Christian love is manifested in seemingly commonplace situations. We rejoice in the virtues and the successes of the beloved, but as a joy for him or her and not for a reassurance that love has not been misplaced. When such reassurance is sought, we can be sure that love is far from perfect. So also we sorrow for weaknesses and sins that can be seen all too clearly, because they are a greater sorrow for the one who has them. If we feel let down by them, love is again imperfect. So far may friendship and heterosexual love attain. Christian love in its perfection is an act of the will, not of the emotions. Nobody can force himself to *like* someone; but he can force himself to *love* in the sense of desiring what is truly best for the other and of doing all in his power to bring that best to pass. Christian love never stops to ask who is worthy of love, since God loves all creatures, and there is not one worthy of the divine love. Christian love does not wave according to the current state of personal relations, or the evidences of whether it is returned. Christian love is perfectly described in the thirteenth chapter of St. Paul's first letter to the Christians who dwelt at Corinth. It would be vain and presumptuous to try to say more about it here, except that no one has ever fully reached that great ideal, but Christians do keep on trying.

Even detached from the tremendous duty of *agape*, human love, in the widest sense that we may give it, does still seem to be the oldest and the most effective answer to our lonely, frightened condition. The Christian will not and need not deny the existence of a special kind of affection for a few people, and the same kind of affection would be felt and acknowledged by the atheist and by any human being whose nature is not strangely warped. The family is a unit which seems almost universal, irrespective of time, place or culture. Even at times of lax or perverted sexuality, an element of affection seems to be indestructible. Its ennobling and liberating influence is feared by those who would like to control men and women completely. Tyrants and their philosophical advisers, from Plato to Hitler, try to kill personal loyalties of love by using external criteria to arrange marriages, permitting promiscuity and homosexuality, making divorce easy and removing children from their parents as early as possible. The breakdown of family life is much deplored today even in countries which claim parliamentary democracy; and there is no doubt that, in rightly providing for those overtaken by misfortune, the state has also made it easier for people to shirk or abandon their responsibilities. But we have discussed the question of loss and gain in modern society already, and found that it does not get very close to our problem. Love remains a reality. The happy family can draw their curtains against the night, and seem to shut out the darkness of the soul as well. The boy and girl returning from the dance can murmur, "I'm not lonely, since I met you." Two close friends can sit together without the need for speech, and silently thank God for granting this breach in the irritations and failures of the day that is past.

To desire any further inquiry might seem to be churlish if not positively ungrateful. The man who wants to analyze human relations must claim the authority of science if he is not to be regarded as something of a monster. The experimental psychologist is tolerated and indeed belauded for his desire to open dark secrets in attitudes and responses which the world generally regards as innocent. The novelist is allowed to dissect his characters, whether with the sharpened clown's wand of Dickens or the clinical scalpel of Joyce. But if we seem to regard love as being under suspicion of falsity like the pools promoter's "membership card," we can hardly escape being accused of misanthropy. Not to accept love, which comes seldom and with difficulty in this world, may seem to range us with the ultimate despair in Sartre's *Huis Clos*: "Hell is other people."

No, love is always good, so long as it is love and not lust or the fruit of any personal gratification. Love that shields from loneliness is good, whether it draws people to cling together in the frightening shadows of the cave or the impersonal roar of the super-factory. But when it is sought for the sake of being a shield, the seeds of evil have entered. It is wrong to use other people as a means to an end, however good that end may empirically seem to be. Once you start thinking of people as a means of saving you from the fear of loneliness, you are no longer loving them as you should. The comparative freedom from loneliness which a full and satisfying life of the affections can give, is by no means to be refused. Yet too often, even in our most sincere love for people, we are influenced by the way in which changes in their circumstances will affect our own. "I hope John doesn't get that job in Manchester, because then I should hardly ever be able to see him." "If Mary fails her exams, she'll be back for another year and I shall be able to go on seeing her." "I could telephone to Bill and see if he's in; but I'm glad he didn't come round last night, because I was awfully tired when I came in." Everyday thoughts, and by no means suggesting that love is insincere. But they do look at things from a subjective point of view, instead of desiring wholeheartedly the good of the beloved. They are only a more adult form of the adolescent boy's fantasy which imagines a desirable girl in some situation where he could prove his heroism and win her gratitude by rescuing her. He would rather that she were in need of his help, at the cost perhaps of her temporary distress, than that she were perfectly happy and in no need of him. And even in later life, we all tend to encourage the breeding of dragons, for the sake of being able to play Perseus or St. George occasionally.

The relationship which offers the greatest dangers of selfishness, and also the highest possibilities of self-sacrifice, is the process of courtship and marriage. Here two people are feeling strong emotion, perhaps for the first time in each of their lives, outside the environment of the families which have filled their consciousness until then. By free choice, they are going to create another such group, to build up something which will be a new force in their society and will be the shaping environment of the new lives which they hope to produce. Now the forces which attract a man and a woman to each other, and which make for a successful marriage, are matters for experts in several fields to consider. One question, however, is raised in the minds of all of us when we look at what our friends and acquaintances are doing in this direction. Are they seeking an escape from loneliness? For it is this loathing of loneliness in the present, or dread of it in the future, which drives many people to think that they might as well get married. It is the force, stronger often than the sex-impulse or the desire to create and protect, which harries the bachelor in his single room and the spinster who is getting tired of asking the other girls in for coffee. It is the threat which has been made against many a young man who looks like slipping out of the engagement. Is this a cynical view? It is not meant to be that, nor to discount the tremendous physical and emotional forces which go to make a marriage. Perhaps once again certain commercial ventures may help us to see the scope of personal attitudes.

Look at the many columns in certain papers which advertise for a meeting with a member of the other sex, "with view to marriage." A great many of these are the hunting-cry of women intent on free gifts and gentle blackmail, and of men who want some cheap sex without any view to marriage at all. Yet many more are heartrendingly sincere; and there are reputable marriage bureaus which do their best to sort out partners on a card index system. Surely this is a strange way of going about something that is one of the most important in the whole of life, and which is hardly to be considered a "natural" one. Perhaps our ideas, long conditioned by a romantic conception of love, are too easily amused or repelled by it. A marriage based on a card index is perhaps at least as likely to succeed as one based on a common liking of a few popular dance tunes. The very existence of advertisements and bureaus for marriage shows how often the accepted system fails. It is amazing to see how many divorced people are coming up quite blandly for the second or third time. Theological opinions apart, one is driven to open-mouthed wonder at their resilience and their capacity always to blame the first failure or two on the partner. Yet though it may sometimes lead to good enough results, this vague casting round for a spouse is selfish in essence. It is the result of a desire to be married, not to find and give happiness with a particular person.

It was a true instinct which led men and women to regard marriage as a great sacred mystery. An equation which defies the normal rules of balance, an exchange in which there is only gain for both, it is surely one of the strangest and most wonderful things in the whole of human life. Something new is created, without loss of that which already existed. A married couple is something more than the sum of its two parts, yet neither the man nor the woman is extinguished as an individual. To say this is, of course, to speak of marriage as it should be, and as it does not invariably turn out in practice. It is a hard task to keep intact the personality which was first loved for itself, to maintain respect for the integrity of the beloved, yet to give and accept such concessions as the changing situation may demand. This continual exchange of courtesy is like an intricate dance, where one is a point of rest around which the partner weaves a figure, but where the pattern is always changing and the roles always being reversed. This is the center of the whole question of love, hardest in marriage where the association is close and constant, but inherent in every human relationship. Unless there is a selfish violence which true love could not tolerate, two distinct personalities remain. Loneliness has to be recognized and shared in two separate but equally conscious manifestations of itself. Neither can lay the whole burden of loneliness on the other, or refuse to share what the other offers.

It is therefore not surprising if deep-rooted selfishness sometimes asserts itself. In face of the apparent impossibility of communication, people come to regard marriage simply as a social convenience, a respectable and regular sexual union, or a means of advancement. The desire of an ambitious young man to improve his position in society by "marrying above his station" is by no means a recent thing. Hogarth's Industrious Apprentice marries his master's daughter, and he is only one of many who reaped this special reward of virtue both in fiction and fact. Whereas it was regarded as a proper thing for the man, the woman was not supposed to get exalted ideas of how she might benefit from marriage. The English novel is strewn with Little Em'lies and Maggie Tullivers who ventured to love where they should not, and ended with neither advancement nor marriage. The idea is strong today, and forms a favorite topic of fanciful conversation among young men who are trying to plan their careers. In recent novels the hero is often shown in search of a rich wife and an influential father-in-law, as a means of getting on in the society which he affects to despise. The young men in books like *Lucky Jim* and *Room at the Top* speak with the true voice of their generation. In a sense they speak also with the voice of the Middle Ages, the convention of courtly love. In the eighteenth-century and Victorian novel, marriage was supposed to be the solution of all problems, including the sexual ones which were hardly mentioned anyway. Today there is a tendency to look on marriage as something apart from love, a contract in which sexual intercourse is only a necessary and somewhat distasteful duty. The raptures of physical love have to be sought outside marriage, and indeed seem to be possible only when marriage is out of the question. It is all very medieval.

Yet if marriage is somewhat despised, sexual love remains one of the most important themes in literature as in life. The Christian can have only one answer to questions about sex outside marriage. It is always wrong, though there are degrees of guilt and no individual has any right to condemn another simply out of his own opinion. Moral theology is, necessarily, a precise subject; its judgments may sometimes seem harsh, but there can be no compromise. The sin is condemned, the sinner may trust in the mercy of God, who is greater than the laws which he has given us to obey. And to go so far as to see all sexual activity as evil, as some Christians in all ages have contrived to do, is to deny God's creation and to stand outside the incarnational mode through which our faith was presented. There is good in whatever proceeds from true love, though the demands of a greater love may call for its physical expression to be consciously withheld. The most cynical of present-day novelists seem to find a certain tenderness in the sexual act and to find in illicit love the joy and comfort which they would deny to marriage.

While it is utterly wrong to regard sex as the work of the devil, it is also wrong to equate the word "love" with sexual intercourse. The equation is made very readily at the present time: proclaimed on posters, shrieked from radios, sobbed into microphones at every dance hall in the country. In the last flickerings of decadent romanticism, the emotions of the individual are exalted into an absolute good, while the real worth of the individual is scorned by this very encouragement to selfishness. Half the popular songs are based on the thinly-veiled assumption that a boy and a girl have recently been in bed together, are about to do so or are somehow cruelly prevented from doing so. Now it is

easy enough to dismiss sex as the mere relief of physical
tension, or to exalt it into a mystique which colors every
human desire and activity. Without going to either
extreme, no consideration of human love and loneliness
can leave out the sexual element. For sex is the fullest
manifestation of giving, of the complete union in which
both give and receive all that can be offered. Two
people, as in the whole marriage partnership, find something greater than the sum of their individual existences,
yet without losing identity. This is again to speak of
the ideal. Sex can also be the worst expression of human
selfishness. It can be brutal, cynical, utterly incon-
siderate of the value of the partner. There are married
couples who treat it in a way that makes the unsanctified
but loving intercourse of adolescents seem almost virtuous. The power of sex is shown in the antitheses which
it creates. It can show man at his noblest, and at his
most contemptible. It can produce utter honesty, when
all the barriers are dropped and two people seem to
know each other's deepest mind through knowledge of
the body; it can also produce arrant hypocrisy, broken
promises, deceits and artifices which are farce on the
stage but tragedy in the home. It can make two people
forget for a time that loneliness has ever touched them; it
can also make loneliness seem intolerable and true contact
further away than ever.

The desire to escape from loneliness, and the continual failure to do so, must be regarded as a most important factor in sexual relationships. Loneliness is perhaps a stronger driving force here than physical desire,

at least so far as sex is sought deliberately and objectively. Prostitution probably would not flourish as it does, at least in its common dingy, furtive, semilegal form, if it did not seem to offer a momentary escape from loneliness. The hungry men who slink, jauntily or with shame, into the known haunts of prostitutes are driven by many things: actual physical desire that they cannot or will not control, the search for a new experience, the joy of being deliberately unfaithful to their wives, the expectation of having something to boast about to the locker-room buddies back home. But mostly they are driven by their loneliness, by the hope that someone will listen and sympathize; deluded by the age-old belief that affection is a marketable commodity. Prostitutes who get their experiences into print always comment on the way in which their "customers" so often seek for tenderness and comfort, and have to be hurried through the act and out into the street as quickly as possible.

Nowhere does the failure of men to find all that they hope for in sex show itself more clearly than in the murky realm of pornography. Raising problems of morality and censorship which are outside our present scope, pornography is also to be seen as a hysterical manifestation of loneliness. It is for those who have failed both to find sexual fulfillment and to come to terms with their situation. Pornography is essentially anti-sex; by trying to create a solitary mental substitute, it destroys the thing with which it claims to be concerned. Its lowest and cheapest levels today treat of almost everything except normal and loving sexual inter-

course. There is violence, brutality, perversion of every
kind. Women seem to be utterly despised and treated
with vicious contempt. For this is the revenge of those
who have failed, and who believe that women have in
fact failed them. Young men singing rude songs in the
bar are expressing the same frustration in a much more
harmless way, destroying by gross ridicule the image
which terrifies them by its beauty. It is easy to condemn
the readers of pornography along with its purveyors.
Stronger than condemnation, there comes a helpless pity
for the loneliness which leads them to such sordid sub-
stitutes. It is the familiar story once again. Human
nature builds up a state of perfect felicity in the imagination; commercial interests batten on this and inflame it.
Men are disappointed because they have hoped more
from sex than can ever be given. They feel excluded
from yet another enchanted garden, and in bitterness
and envy their sense of loneliness is increased.

This is all a very dark side of the picture, but one
which cannot be left out or passed over casually. Does
it seem now to the reader as if the Christian writer
were up to his old tricks, condemning every sign of
human joy, and the sexual ones above all others? Is this
just another way of driving men to repentance through
despair? Let us take a look at the brighter side, and
see whether the enchanted garden is always an illusion.
Right-thinking men do not have to hold any special
position of faith to agree that prostitution, pornography
and so on are bad and that they fail to solve the problems which drive men to seek them. Yet there are many

happy marriages, in which sex does provide both a mutual expression of love and a height of joy which the most fervid brain could never imagine. And sex apart, there are friendships where there is no thought of loss or gain, but only pleasure in the existence of each other in a shared situation. Two personalities seem to merge into one, yet without loss of either. The sense of regard is no longer objective: there is some difference between the relationships "he and I" and "we."

Human love is the nearest we have come so far to finding a solution to the problem of human loneliness. It is probably as far as we can ever get within our general environment and material resources. Indeed there is something which seems to rise out of this world altogether in the fact that loneliness can be exchanged and shared. It is something that defeats reason, to know that two separate human beings can become so close. All the frustrations and failures, the cold silences, the inability to communicate, are swept away in the miracle of complete understanding. For it is a miracle, none the less so for being as old as mankind and yet continually renewed. It is far beyond our reasonable expectation or our deserving. The mind can more easily conceive of a world without any loving contact than a world where love is supreme and unbroken; poetic descriptions of hell are always more lively than those of heaven, and it is our own failure to love that makes us fail also to realize the energy that God's love pours into us as we get closer to him. As for our deserving, the most arrogant of men can be humbled by a sense of their unworthiness to receive the love that is given.

This is the great hope of the rationalist or humanist. Ever since cracks appeared in the orthodox tower, men have been troubled by the problem of ethics without faith. Many who felt themselves honestly unable to accept the doctrines of Christianity still recognized that Christian morality had worked for good in the world. What would happen when, as they then believed probable, all men turned away from Christianity? Would the beast be set free and anarchy prevail? Searching their own deepest experiences, they found that love was to be the answer. The natural affections in men were blunted but not destroyed by the conditions of a material and increasingly affluent society. If men could be taught to love one another, if the opportunity for disinterested service could be put before them, all might yet be well. The simple innocence of children offered such an opportunity, and a reminder of what was truly in man but so soon forgotten. Scrooge and Silas Marner could be converted, and all must follow their example or perish. Although some have shown themselves more likely to put Tiny Tim into a gas chamber for being a cripple than to cherish him, the faith in the remedial power of human affection remains. What does the Christian say about it? Does he regard it as untrue, or as irrelevant? His view of human love is the highest that can be conceived. Knowing the evil and corruption in men, seeing clearly his own continual failure to fulfill the call to universal love, the Christian must surely be amazed at the way in which people can triumph over themselves. That people can get so close in love, is another gift of that divine Love who cares so much for grubby, limited human beings that he came to be one among them.

So we might seem to be near agreement on the solution to our problem of loneliness. Though human relationships are always imperfect and the depths of affection are not very often attained, yet at least we might seem to have an ideal toward which to strive. If we all loved one another as we should, the will of God would be fulfilled here on earth. The humanist's dream would also be fulfilled, through the working of that religion which he had tried to destroy and yet feared to lose. Would we be free from loneliness? Could love bring about such a change in the whole human condition that this deep anxiety and sense of separation would no longer exist?

If the answer is not hopeful, this is not because of the recognized imperfections in love as we now experience it. It goes far below the surface of relationships which are to some extent conditioned by the time and place in which they exist, and reaches something inherent in the whole idea of love. For though love "seeketh not itself to please," as Blake wrote, and though love is concerned to give rather than to receive, it is nevertheless conscious of its existence. Two personalities may draw so close that a new entity has indeed been created, but by the enrichment and not the extinction of each individual. A love relationship is possible because each personality is unique and therefore lonely. If all were merged in one gigantic "world-soul," it would not be love as we can venture to use the word now, for it is the distinctions between people that make it possible to give, to receive, even to recognize love. And once love is recognized, the lover is once more the self-conscious observer of self. Not through vanity, but through the nature of being, nobody can ever get a completely objective picture of the world in which he is living; for the attempt to observe means the conscious withdrawal of himself from the picture, which is thus no longer complete. So the lover may lose himself for a few moments in the relationship of love, but if he is going to play his part in that relationship so that it may endure, he must become aware of it and therefore partially withdraw from it. It is only out of his loneliness that he can contribute to the unfolding of love. There is a paradox in love, which demands and yet forbids a complete giving. Though one may want to sink his personality completely in that of the beloved, it may not be done. To lose all that marks out the individual would be to lose the things which cause love. Neither in sacrifice nor for refuge can the lover become less than his full self.

So there is no refuge here either, though there is comfort. Love can assuage loneliness, more fully than anything else on earth can do. Not only the physical condition of being alone, but the deeper and darker anxieties can be relieved by marriage, family, friendship and all the many ways in which we think of love. Yet perfect though the relationship may sometimes seem to be, it always carries within itself the beginning of the end.

Death puts a stop to all love that we know in this world. In every relationship it is certain, except for some rare chance, that one of the partners will die before the other. One must suffer loss and learn to live without the physical presence that had previously seemed essential to life. And though love can and does continue to have its power after death, there is yet a new and terrible loneliness which nothing can remove. The greatest relief from loneliness also prepares the way for the worst loneliness perhaps which we can know. We know this, and enter no less willingly into loving. The greatest tribute that love can pay will come after the death of the beloved. Loneliness can be borne as a price for the other's happiness. The survivor can thank God that the dead one is beyond all pain and danger, untouched by the perils that life must bring. Above all, the one who remains alone can feel thankful for being allowed to bear the loneliness which one or the other was bound to feel. This intense loneliness is transformed and made a cause for rejoicing, since the other has gone first and not been made to bear the loss.

The more we pursue and investigate loneliness, the more deeply in our condition it seems to be rooted. At the very heart of love, when loneliness seems to be removed, we find that a new loneliness is being prepared. The loneliness of bereavement, the most feared and perhaps the most terrible type of loneliness, can become the most glorious. The Christian can rejoice even in his sorrow, since he believes that the dead are wonderfully and eternally blessed. Even without this

faith, the acceptance of loneliness can be made a cause
of rejoicing that the other has not had to make that
acceptance.

Perhaps acceptance is the answer, since every attempt
to flee from loneliness seems only to increase both its
actual and its potential force. Is it to be a grudging
acceptance, regarding loneliness as an encumbrance and
an imperfection; or is it possible to find something con-
structive in so doing? Must loneliness be dragged around
like a wooden leg, or is it possible to use it as a staff
and a weapon in our struggle? We are not far from
trying to find that answer, but there is another road
that has to be tried first. It is a dark and dangerous
road, but many have chosen it and we must follow them
for a little way.

8

MAN ALONE

WHEN MAN is driven hard enough, he may show either the weakest or the bravest of the beast that is in him. Pushed beyond hope, he will lose all resistance and wait to be torn to pieces, or he will stand at bay and refuse to give in while he still has claws and teeth. Recognition of his plight, and of the ultimate inadequacy of the many attempts to escape from it, has often sent him groveling to the earth with no more fight left in him. Others have found the greatest defiance in despair. If loneliness can never be removed, they say, let it be accepted and even welcomed. Since all that society, love and friendship can offer do not reach to the heart, we will refuse them all. Man reaches his true stature only when he can stand alone, when he is free from all attachments. The proud cry, *non serviam*, is one of the oldest, a stubborn glorying in loneliness and a denial of any commitment to others. Since society cannot release us from the anxiety of being a thinking individual, we contract out of society. Since God has laid on us the burden of choice through free will, we choose freely to reject him. Old and constantly renewed, the refusal

to compromise is often heard today. It may be the bitter
selfishness of a Mordred:

> I will have my choice, and be adored for the having;
> when my father King Arthur has fallen in the wood of
> his elms,
> I will sit here alone in a kingdom of Paradise.[1]

or the fierce integrity of a Stephen Daedalus:

> You have asked me what I would do and what I would
> not do. I will tell you what I will do and what I will not
> do. I will not serve that in which I no longer believe,
> whether it call itself my home, my fatherland or my
> church; and I will try to express myself in some mode of
> life or art as fully as I can and as cunningly as I can, using
> for my defence the only arms I allow myself to use—
> silence, exile and cunning.[2]

It is the cry of many ordinary men and women, bitter
or resigned, hysterical or at peace with themselves, who
look at all kinds of authority and association only to
decide "it's not for me."

Here again, the Romantic movement may be seen as
initiating some new and unfortunate tendencies, in addi-
tion to reviving many that had been in abeyance for a
while. The young radicals who defied church and state
alike in their new-found enthusiasm for the essential
goodness of man, found themselves at odds with the
whole society around them. Distrusted by ordinary
respectable people, as well as by politicians and prelates,
they soon decided that they might as well be hanged

[1] Charles Williams, "The Meditation of Mordred" in *The Region
of the Summer Stars.*

[2] James Joyce, *Portrait of the Artist as a Young Man,* chapter 5.

for a red-blooded sheep of practice as for an anemic lamb of theory. Often justifying Canning's sneer that political reform went along with "gay morality and easy vice," they yet found a certain nobility and even purity through the intensity with which they refused to compromise. The untidy hair and the open collar instead of the starched cravat, were symbols of freedom no less potent than loose sweaters and tight trousers seem to have become more recently.

The Romantic poets were born to tragedy in their lives. Keats, who shared so little in the wilder political aspirations, found his own freedom before he coughed himself to death at twenty-six. Shelley's drowned beauty was burned in a wild, pagan pyre on the Italian shore before he was thirty. Byron died in the incoherent, jealous scramble for Greek independence, heroically leaving a life that had contained little heroism and that cast its shadow for a generation or more to come. Coleridge sank into opium-stupefied oblivion. Wordsworth, perhaps the most tragic of them all, lived to be eighty, to be Victoria's Poet Laureate and to hold a sinecure under the Crown that he had once longed to shake and overthrow. All of them knew in special measure that the human condition is inescapably lonely, and all found at some time that the essence of poetry could be found in loneliness. Keats drops back from the bliss of the nightingale's ascent to an earth where there is no security and no abiding love. Shelley's Alastor sails away to enchanted lands and leaves the world behind. Byron, above all, found his heroes in the solitary,

the wanderer, the deliberate outsider. His Don Juan,
Childe Harold, Cain, Manfred and the rest continued to
stalk defiantly about Europe long after he was dead,
bearing the legend that makes him in German eyes the
second English poet after Shakespeare.

The rise and development of this aspect of Romanticism, and the nemesis which it must bring upon itself,
is shown most plainly of all in Mary Shelley's *Frankenstein*. The daughter of William Godwin, the exponent
of perfectibility, and of Mary Wolstonecraft who was
an outspoken defender of women's rights, she became
Shelley's second wife and thus linked the two generations
of the English Romantics. *Frankenstein* was written in
1816 in Switzerland, to pass away part of a rainy summer
spent there with her husband and Byron. The theme
is well known and has been used in many garbled forms
since. The idea of a young experimenter who creates
a monster from bits of human bodies, only to find that
he has set free a hideous thing of great strength which
he cannot control, is typical of the vogue for horror
and supernatural thrills which is a recurring strain in
the English novel and a feature of Romanticism itself.
The interesting quality of the book is the character of
the monster himself. At first full of sweetness and love
because he has known no corruption—the splendid
savage again—he is spurned by those whose society he
seeks. Forced to observe happy families from outside,
envying the innocent children who flee in terror at his
approach, he gradually turns from noble humanity to
the full force of the beast. After a series of brutal

killings, the strangely articulate monster speaks with a mixture of defiance, self-pity and self-abhorrence:

> Once my fancy was soothed with dreams of virtue, of fame and of enjoyment. Once I falsely hoped to meet with beings who, pardoning my outward form, would love me for the excellent qualities which I was capable of unfolding. I was nourished with high thoughts of honor and devotion. But now crime has degraded me beneath the meanest animal. No guilt, no mischief, no malignity, no misery, can be found comparable to mine. When I run over the frightful catalog of my sins, I cannot believe that I am the same creature whose thoughts were once filled with sublime and transcendent visions of the beauty and the majesty of goodness. But it is even so; the fallen angel becomes a malignant devil. Yet even that enemy of God and man had friends and associates in his desolation; I am alone.

"I am alone"; so lies the story of Romanticism, from the gentle tears over spring flowers to the shrieks of Europe in flames. So speaks the delinquent who swears that he meant well, until people laughed at his hair style and pointed shoes and thus made him into a killer. Recognizing the existence of good, yet refusing to embrace it except on his own terms, the monster still walks; the proud figure of Man Alone has shrunk to the lonely man.

The cult of solitariness has tinged so much of our thought and practice over the last hundred and fifty years that it is important to look at some of the forms in which it has emerged. It was an easy declension from the cult of pure emotion, uncontrolled by sterile reason, to the cult of any emotion whatever provided it was big enough. Admiration for the man who defied tyranny led to admiration for the man who defied any aspect of existing authority. Cheers for the radical leader swelled to yells for the leader of any kind, irrespective of where he was going. The post-Romantic hero can be studied in the pages of the Brontë sisters, whose Rochesters and Heathcliffes are Byronic figures inflamed and inflated by the imagination of passionate girls who had no hope of living fully in the great world. To say that their inspiration here was literary, is not of course to deny their great genius or the true humanity that also appears. Napoleon passed from archvillain to supreme hero almost before he was dead, and his image haunted many nineteenth-century writers. Byron, indeed, had perversely desired a Napoleonic victory and greeted the news of Waterloo with, "I'm damned sorry for it." For Napoleon, surrounded though he was by his staff and his loyal soldiers, was yet a great solitary, an outsider. Like Cain and the rest, he chose to accept and develop the power that he felt within himself, following its course, though he might be led to what lesser men would consider cruel, unjust and immoral. That quality in Napoleon which Goethe described to Eckermann as "daemonic" found approval in later generations who longed for a Superman to lead them out of their barren present. Carlyle looked upon the great in all fields as heroes. Rising nationalism all over Europe called for heroes; in due time they got Bismarck, and Hitler, and Mussolini and Stalin.

The demand for a leader turned inward as well. The individual who was at odds with society, seeing no escape from his gnawing loneliness, started to look for the same qualities within himself. "If there is to be a leader, why should not I be that one? If I cannot lead nations, surely I can lead myself." So, the master of his fate, each man could be his own Napoleon if he chose to be equally heedless of conventional restraints. The little Napoleon had to prove himself in some way, to be big in some kind of villainy. Not for everyone was the massacre of the Peninsular War, not indeed the black arts of Manfred or the monumental lecheries of Don Juan. But the humblest solitary could set himself apart from unsympathetic society by cutting a throat or perpetrating a few minor cruelties. To be a failed Napoleon seemed better than to suffer without protest. If strength is lacking, ambition and resolution can still avail the man who has courage to set himself apart from the herd and say, "Evil, be thou my good." The type can be studied in the character of Raskolnikov in Dostoevsky's *Crime and Punishment*. Poor and lonely, Raskolnikov dares himself to be more than human by denying the moral standard by which other men live. His demonstration is no great battle, but the murder for theft of an old pawnbroker. He convinces himself that he is entitled to her money, can do more good with it than she ever will. But at last he is forced to admit that he killed for the sense of power which it gave him, for the sake of proving to himself that he was not as other men. He even compares himself with Napoleon who "storms Toulon, orders a massacre in Paris, forgets an army in Egypt, wastes half a million men in the Moscow ex-

pedition and gets off with a jest at Vilna." Yet Raskolnikov has misjudged himself. He suffers the remorse of
guilt and breaks down under the assertive power of those
qualities of decency and compassion which he had striven
to deny. At last he is more lonely and insecure than
he had ever been before, uncertain even of the reality
of his own individual self.

The will to power is thus a two-edged weapon which
is liable to turn against its bearer. The attempt to live
on a big scale may make a man realize how small he
really is. The Superman continues to patrol the frontiers
of the human mind, but he is an increasingly lachrymose
and self-pitying Superman. His insecurity grows as he
sees on the one side that cosy if petty society which
he has sworn to quit for ever, and on the other a desert
whose bounds are not within sight. In popular art he
remains as a symbol of the age-old desire to be different,
to be larger than life. Books and films revel in the hero-
villain, regarded by society as a criminal but devoted
to a justice which is greater than the justice of the police
courts; an old figure in a new guise. Robin Hood now
carries a revolver instead of a bow, and smokes continual
cigarettes as he wisecracks his way through scenes of
violence to a climax that brings him out on top of cops
and robbers alike. To be above both good and evil as
this world understands them is one of man's oldest
dreams. There is something sweet in the word "outlaw."
He who turns his back on society in a fit of pique can
always say, like Frankenstein's monster, that society
failed to recognize the sweetness of his nature. It says

much for the natural sense of the human race that the
concept of Superman has become something of a joke
among readers of popular science fiction. The most
successful works in this field are those which show quite
ordinary people thrown into strange events and develop-
ing a heroism that is within social values instead of
deliberately outside them.

Yet the solitary instincts may be cultivated without
trying to emulate either Napoleon or Robin Hood.
Rejection of restraint may keep within the law, and may
even keep within the limits of the individual mind.
Conscious of being unique and lonely, men refuse to
admit the validity of any system. That which comes
from outside cannot touch the real being: "The mind is
its own place." Christianity in particular is rejected
because it offers a pattern by which men should live.
The idea of atonement and redemption is utterly foreign
to the solitary. He did not ask to be placed in this
predicament and he does not ask to be pulled out of it.
Set here in a wilderness where there can be no communication, he scorns the gestures and mouthings by
which men try to pretend that they can understand each
other. There is no salvation except what a man may
create for himself. A man may create an empire in his
own head and rule there supreme. Well, so he may;
but the effort is liable to crack his skull from within in
spite of every effort that he makes to stop it being
cracked from without. Whatever can be thus created
is largely dependent on others. Imagination needs something to work on, and the images, the concepts, the

very words that describe them, have all been taught through life in society and the exchange of ideas. There can be no true solitary except a child cast alone on a desert island, and therefore not surviving. The result of locking the brain once it is well stored is decadence—both in the moral and the intellectual sense. Images ferment together until they burst out in madness. Dorian Gray lingers and broods over strange sensations like a miser over his gold, and the end is degenerate death.

Again, the desire to be an outsider may show itself in a feverish pursuit after pleasure. Other people are only half alive, but the real man must taste everything life has to offer. Only through continual excess can he find freedom from the limited human condition and rise to a height of understanding which enables him to be free of restraint: he must feast one day and fast the next, must be a libertine and a celibate, a sadist and a giver of charity. Nothing is "good" or "bad"; there are only possible sensations and a man must experience them all. Bondage lies in choice according to the standards of society. For the free man, it is enough to know that something is possible in order to experience it. So specialization is to be condemned, or rather we must live so as to be specialists in everything. This impossible task was approved by a great many thinkers, including Goethe. It invaded the Aesthetic school of writers in England at the end of the nineteenth century. Pater was ecstatic in his belief that "Not the fruit of experience, but experience itself is the end." [3] Lawrence

[3] Walter Pater, "Conclusion" to *The Renaissance* (1868).

was for the life of the senses lived without inhibition or petty restraint; and Aldous Huxley has looked both satirically and favorably on the idea of the "complete man."

We are offered, then, a solution to our problem. Since we are to be lonely, let us turn in on our loneliness and create from it images to give us company that flesh and blood cannot give. If there is no communication with other people, if religion is just one of the restraints which society lays upon us in the attempt to reconcile us to further restraint, can we do better than live the artificial life of the senses? Is art the only way of liberation, imposing a pattern on inchoate life, helping us by making us concentrate on our individual perception? Perhaps, like the Michael Robartes of Yeats, each of us can inhabit his solitary house and enjoy the company of dead beauty, called up from the past. Perhaps the only refuge from our sickness is with those who have already passed beyond its reach.

Perhaps not, for ancient beauty does not come to us on fairy wings but through the sweating hands of men and women who did not try to slip away from the struggle. The existence of art is a constant proof that some communication is possible, that wisdom and courage can be seized and handed on so that the struggle may continue. The cultivation of the solitary instincts must end in sterility, whether through crimes that cut a man off from his fellows or through the refusal to live as a full, suffering member of the human race. Yet it is seldom such a positive thing, but rather the peevish

withdrawal from a game that is being played by un-
desired rules. The solitary man is identified by sour
grapes more often than by the heady fermentations of
Bacchic orgies. He is like the child who cannot order
games in the playground at his own will, and then runs
away saying that he does not want to play and would
rather be alone. Renunciation may be a great virtue,
but there is little merit in deciding to be solitary when
other people have already decided that they do not want
anything to do with you. The type of the solitary is
very often not Michael Robartes but Leopold Bloom.
Nobody has expressed better than Joyce the drifters and
exiles, washed up on dead-ends of the world. European
Jewish by origin, an Irish citizen, baptized in a Protes-
tant church, conforming to Roman Catholic worship,
personally agnostic, Bloom sums up in himself the frag-
mentation of modern man. Betrayed by his wife and
despised by most of the men he knows, he is unable to
form any real attachments of love or friendship. Fearful
of plunging to the depths of aberration which his in-
telligent mind offers, he is pathetic yet by no means
contemptible. He can feel affection and compassion and
exercise a gentle humor. Yet society seems to have no
place for him and the result is not a noble withdrawal
but mere sterility. The great outsider is reduced in the
twentieth century to Leopold Bloom masturbating on
the beach near Dublin; and the great satanic blasphemies
are reduced to rude jokes about the vicar.

Since the Leopold Blooms are many and yet not contemptible, we cannot assume that the outsider is always

wrong any more than some have assumed that he is always right. We have already seen what pressures to conform are laid upon the individual today, and how often they are accepted in the vain faith that they will somehow dispel the loneliness which the individual feels. We live at a time when "anti-social" is a very pejorative term. Those who are so labelled are sometimes the finest types, ostracized by the group in which they have to live because their standards resist the pressures. Those who are most alert and conscious of the implications of what is going on, may be the strongest opposers of the prevailing ethos. This can be seen in any community, whether of schoolboys, students, soldiers, workers or a parish club. The pattern is often stamped by a few, perhaps lovers of power or perhaps believing that they know best for the group, and is reproduced at every level. It takes a perceptive man to see possible flaws in that pattern and a brave one to point them out. Nobody wants to be told that the emperor has no clothes. Unable to make their opinions felt, perhaps even persecuted by the ruling clique, these critics soon find themselves psychically outside the group within which they must physically remain. They withdraw from communal activities and walk alone.

The outsider may not even be opposed to the patterns of his group, but may be impelled by a sense of inadequacy. Genuine humility exists, and there are people who can say "I am not worthy," and mean it; though there are many more who will say it only so that they may be asked a second and a third time. There are others who feel inadequate to take a full part in the activities that so delight others, not from a sense of humility but from a variety of causes, often deep-seated ones. While a sense of unworthiness is highly proper in every human relationship, it can become dangerously inhibiting. The types who withdraw from participation for this reason are many. There are some who are perfectionists, who will not take part in anything unless they can win. Others, without demanding supremacy, fear that they will be shown up as less competent than their fellows. It is always pleasant to be able to say, "I could have done that if I'd tried," and a lot of people go on saying it all their lives without ever taking the risk of trying. Some have had to struggle so much to enter the group that they are terrified of slipping back out of it. Like men on a raft they will lie still on the slippery edge, because the heave to get to the center might tip them into the sea. Some again, like those deceived by advertisements, have built up a false image of the group so glorious that the failure to realize it seems to be attributable only to their own weakness. They will not stoop to drink from the humble well because a lovely mirage still beckons them on.

Whatever the causes, and however deserving of compassion the resistant individual may be, the judgments of Cain and of Frankenstein's lachrymose monster still rest on those who willfully choose to be apart. How can they be distinguished from the true rebel, the man who follows his conscience wherever it leads, the rebel without whom society would grind to a stop from inertia? Is the martyr only another Manfred? By actions and not by words is the way to judge. The objector for the sake of conscience is so consumed by his cause that it enters into everything he does. If the group casts him out, he will continue to write and preach and scream the truth of what he believes. He works continually to convert others to the cause. He is silenced by neither promises nor threats. Whether he is right or wrong—and sincerity is unfortunately no guarantee of accuracy—the genuine objector is wholeheartedly active. The other outsider reacts differently to his position. He usually becomes slothful, taking no interest in what is going on, not even communicating with other members of the group. He seeks to live in his own world, neither needing nor inviting the attentions of others. When he is moved to expression or action, it is usually in a manic way, for some minor grievance or impossible project. He will not support any cause that wins popular approval, but only something dredged up from his solitude and having relevance to nothing but his own unhappiness. Anyone who has had to lead or organize any kind of group will recognize the type, and knows his exasperating need for compassion and help.

The condemnation of the withdrawal which is the result of temper rather than conscience is in the condition itself. It is self-perpetuating: once a man has cut himself off, the factors which caused him to do so will become steadily worse. Lacking faith in a greater good to sustain him, he hates the weakness and yet cherishes it. Any change of heart, even when one is desired, is resisted because it would seem a sign of weakness. There must be no compromise toward a return once the retreat has been made. We all know the condition in its simpler forms: the child who has been naughty and refuses all offers of reconciliation; the lovers who stay silent and apart after a quarrel in order to punish the other, though each heart is sad with longing; the committee member who refuses to withdraw the motion that is making him unpopular, though he himself is already sick of it. Once a man has done wrong so that he will not be thought weak, the initial fear is increased and drives him on to worse deeds. And to see the opposition that he has created gives him a sense of power. Those who have failed to inspire love may get a great deal of satisfaction from inspiring hate. Evil is not creative, but it can appear to be so by breaking up the existing pattern and thrusting back toward chaos.

It is indeed a dark road. The man who recognizes the essential loneliness of his whole journey is wiser than those who huddle together and sing songs in the hope that loneliness will thus be destroyed. But wisdom accepts the fellowship and the singing for good in themselves, and does not throw them back with a curse. If the road is dark, it is folly to pretend that the sun is shining; but it is also folly to blow out the lantern because it is not so bright as the sun. The man who insists on standing apart creates around him an attitude of repulsion and suspicion which aggravates more than his own trouble. He has the right to choose for himself, but also the duty to consider the consequences of his choice for others; and that is what the deliberately outside never do consider. Each of us is made to some extent by his environment, and to break away from that environment is to do some violence both to it and to ourselves. If the cause is good, the violence may be justified; but too often there is no spring of action but pique, resentment and selfishness. From Satan down to his newest disciple, the refusal to serve which begins with a mighty shaking of fists always ends up in a petulant biting of nails.

We have pursued lonely man to the edge of the abyss, and refused to allow him to take refuge even in his own loneliness. He is told not to depend on the group, yet not to forsake it. His burden seems heavier than ever, his anxiety more featureless, his nakedness more complete. Is there no comfort?

9

LEAP IN THE DARK

IN LOOKING at the many lines of retreat which men have created for themselves or have had laid open before them, and no less in looking at the many kinds of resistance which they have put up against the encroachment of loneliness, one particular commitment has never been far away. Christianity keeps appearing in all these discussions, pushed out of the way when one path is being followed only to reappear on a new one. The guides on false escape routes have tried to explain away Christianity, to enlist some aspects of it on their side, or simply to suppress knowledge of its existence. The nobler rebels have often seen in Christianity the worst enemy of man's freedom, itself offering a false escape when in fact we should turn and bravely face our predicament. Christianity is denied because it poses awkward questions about comparative values, and refuses to allow any man to claim superiority over the human situation. It is also denied because it offers comfort and a hope of alleviating that situation. Paradoxes have a habit of holding truth somewhere at their center. We have found that there is no running away from loneliness, because it is an inner condition of the individual, which external circumstances can ease or worsen but never remove. Perhaps we might look at this extra element which has kept cropping up all the time.

It would be tedious to pretend that Christian claims are unknown in the countries of the West today. Although those claims are so widely rejected, the modern Christian faces his missionary duty on a different level from that of the first Christians, or of earlier missionaries to distant parts of the world. There is a great deal of misunderstanding, old legends still believed, rejections without proper examination, repetition of crass attacks that are dead issues. A tragically large number of children and young people know the names and themes of Christianity only as a joke, an oath, or at most a vague accompaniment to certain social occasions. Nevertheless, we do not live in an age or a place where the Christian church has never existed. This is a post-Christian society, where certain Christian values have been accepted and put into practice even though no attention is given to their origin. Our culture has developed out of centuries when Christianity was accepted and, at least in its public worship, almost universally practiced. Without making elaborate statements about an "age of faith," and certainly without claiming that conduct in every aspect has deteriorated with the passing of time, it cannot be denied that this country and many others would be different if Christianity had never been taught within them. The unbeliever today is not a man who has never heard of the Christian God. He is one who has chosen the way of rejection: he has in effect said to Christ, "I want nothing to do with you."

However he may protest about it, this is the truth. I speak not of the Jew, the Moslem, the Buddhist, or any who follow a life of religious faith and practice which for them must exclude the unique claim of Christianity. It is the ordinary man, considering himself a decent enough chap as he reads his evening paper after a hard day's work to sustain his family, who is a good neighbor in the matter of borrowed lawn mowers, who drinks little and swears less—it is he who has looked on the face of Christ and turned away. We live in a world where Christ continually challenges us. Whatever disputes on detail there may be, whatever past and present iniquities may be blamed on those who call themselves Christians, the fact remains. A man has claimed to be divinely appointed to teach and to be himself divine; his life has been proclaimed as the one historical life which resolves the predicament of all other lives; his personal survival of bodily death has been the basis of faith for his contemporary friends and for millions thereafter. These things can be laughed to scorn, explained away, utterly refused; but nothing can be the same again since they have happened. And the refusal to choose, as we saw earlier, is a rejection. Intellectual arguments about first principles, philosophical proofs of the existence of God as a logical necessity, are secondary to the very early Christian baptismal confession, "I believe that Jesus Christ is the Son of God." This is not a question of Christian arrogance;

simply, such words have been said and everyone who is aware of them must make up his own mind before he can embroil himself in religious discussions. The Jew who says clearly, "Jesus Christ is not the Son of God, because God is of such a nature that he will not be thus limited and contained, suffering all human pains in a life that ended in execution for blasphemy," is in a position to command Christian respect. The man who says, "First prove to me that there is a God," has already rejected the Christian message. He has a right to do so; God has given him the free will with which to do so. All we ask of him is that he shall not, after this rejection, claim to have an open mind about Christianity, or to be a Christian in his own way, or to be a better Christian than people who go regularly to church. He may be a better man than many churchgoers, but he is not a better Christian and he ought not to try to have it both ways.

It is not enough to have heard the Christian words. Those words, like all words, are mere waves in the air or marks on a piece of paper until they are received by an individual mind. There is no merit in sitting in a church and letting the words flow over you, without fastening on to what they contain that is relevant to your own individual situation. The opponents who accuse Christians of going to church once a week and showing no signs in their lives of what they hear there, have a shrewd and too often genuine ground for attack. This is no new thing; Christ compared preaching to the man sowing seed by the old method of scattering it

in all directions over the field, so that only a little took
root and escaped the perils of stones, thorns and de-
vouring birds. Wherever he went the crowds pressed
around him, impatient to see some demonstration of
power or to hear some clever saying; yet he knew at
once when a woman touched his clothes with faith that
she could thus be cured. His disciples were amazed,
but he knew that one touch of faith amid all the jostling
of curiosity, and so it is still. Theologians who have
insisted on the supreme importance of the individual
encounter between God and man have stated a vital
truth, even though their further deductions have sometimes been unsound. We cannot afford to discount the
objective records by which the encounter is mediated,
otherwise we are left with nothing more than a vague
Wordsworthian sense of "something far more deeply
interfused." The true encounter, however it may be
outwardly recognizable, is more than one observable
phenomenon among many. It is an act of creation,
unique and incommunicable, because it speaks directly
from God to a man's loneliness.

Since choice is thus demanded, are we to assume that
a man can find God by seeking? To put it more per-
tinently, could the splendid savage on his lonely island,
deduce by the exercise of reason the whole Christian
story and come at last to intellectual acceptance of its
implications? This is clearly not true; if it were, the
objective, historical fact of Christ's incarnation and all
that followed would be unnecessary. Indeed, it was
just this sense of wastefulness which "dis-commended"

Christianity to some tidy-minded thinkers of the eighteenth and nineteenth centuries who held that every man could attain to God in his own way, by the light of reason. God reaches out to each one of us, inviting but not forcing the response of acceptance. We can make no progress of ourselves, but we can resist progress. The lifeline swings above the dark waters, but we continue to claw at the slippery sides of the dock in proud determination to find our own way out. It is not a question of choice between an easy and a hard way of rescue. Without the lifeline there is no hope of getting out, and the lifeline itself demands a firm grasp and bleeding hands if it is to be effective. The hands that hold the other end are bleeding, too, for they are the hands of a God who, through the miraculous self-limiting of himself, has felt the same loneliness which now afflicts us. It is because loneliness is thus shared, to a degree which no rationalist philosopher could ever think out, that we are no better than drowning men unless we are willing to accept the sharing of the burden. To give your loneliness into the hands of Christ is to take upon you something of his loneliness too.

All this is not for the "religious" in either the technical or the popular sense of that word. Christ had no particular liking for "religious" people when he walked on earth, and indeed gave them some of his most severe words. Ah, says the "better Christian than those who go to church," just so; now withdraw those harsh words a few pages ago. But what Christ demanded was acceptance of his words and his unique person, and the complete change of personality which should follow that acceptance. The offer was made freely to each in his situation. That situation included, and still includes for every one of us, the power of the individual to exercise his free choice. The love of God is a fire that spreads while there is the slightest fuel for it to consume. It is like a hound that never gives up the scent, whatever refuge may be sought, as Francis Thompson knew in his long attempt to escape:

> I fled Him down the nights and down the days,
> I fled Him down the arches of the years,
> I fled Him down the labyrinthine ways
> Of my own mind; and in the midst of tears
> I fled from Him, and under running laughter.
>   Up vistaed hopes I sped;
>   And shot, precipitated
> Adown Titanic glooms of chasmèd fears,
> From those strong Feet that followed, followed after.[1]

But when the quarry is cornered at last, the surrender must be complete and willed. God's love never leaves go until the individual has looked straight at it and pushed it away. The rejection is our own choice, and we must abide by it. The acceptance is our own choice too, but we can feel no merit in accepting what is freely given. We fail to realize the all-embracing power of God, which gives us even the will to accept or to reject if we think of the situation simply as a bargain to be struck by two independent parties agreeing on terms. It is important to remember that

> Whatever good there is in our lives and actions (and it is but fragmentary) is "all of God," and it was His before it

[1] Francis Thompson, "The Hound of Heaven."

was ours, was divine grace before it was human achievement, is indeed a matter of God taking up our poor human nature into union with His own divine life, making us more truly personal, yet also more disposed to ascribe it all to Him.[2]

That there is a flight, even by those who most desire to love God, cannot be denied. God gives us the power to flee, and we exercise it all too readily; either in minor scurryings away from understood duty at moments when it seems inconvenient, or in a steady cross-country trot that ensures we shall always be just too far away to hear the words. For the flight is a flight of the will, rather than of the reason and intellect. Unbelievers arguing against Christianity often paint pathetic little pictures of themselves and their friends as people who desperately want to believe but are held back by honest doubts. We are supposed to imagine them in long sleepless vigils, trying so hard to believe the beautiful story but always forced by terrific intellectual integrity to say "No." I beg leave to share some of their own skepticism and question whether this is really what happens. There are always a few perhaps who somehow cannot believe though they desire to do so, "wingless birds" as Hardy movingly described them, himself among them. But the long vigils of doubt are better known to those like Hopkins who

> That night, that year
> Of now done darkness I wretch lay wrestling with
> (my God!) my God.[3]

[2] D. M. Baillie, *God Was in Christ* (New York: 1948), p. 117.
[3] Gerard Manley Hopkins, "Carrion Comfort."

For there is plenty of room, perhaps necessity, for honest doubt after the acceptance; faith is no faith if the possibility of being wrong is not there as a solemn bass to the joyful melody. But there is little evidence of people brooding over details, in an effort to get everything resolved and dropped neatly into place before becoming converted. If there are such, they have never known the beginning of faith; any more than a man who wants to be satisfied about every detail of a woman's character and habits before he marries her has known even the beginning of love.

The fact is that the only desire which many people feel toward Christianity is the desire to share the softer parts of it and contract out of the difficult bits. There are some who, more nobly, refuse even the comfort and would rather suffer alone than seek any change in their conditions. But many will not choose because they fear the consequences of choice. Every person who is not a Christian should ask himself honestly whether he holds back because acceptance would mean radical and inconvenient changes in his life. It may be some clear and palpable inconvenience, such as giving up a cosy state of adultery that is currently being enjoyed; or getting up early more often, in order to go to church. Plenty of men will argue against Christianity in the bar on a Saturday night, secure in the knowledge that it is not going to interfere with their pleasures next day. It may be not any particular vice or indulgence, but the whole freedom of choice that they fear to lose. For one who is not a Christian because he has doubts about Cain's wife, there are thousands who simply want to go on doing exactly as they like.

We have seen how men, for a long time now and still today, have asserted the rights of the individual over all possible systems. Many of the noblest minds have refused to accept any will but their own, and Christianity has often been lumped together with systems designed simply for the oppression and exploitation of the people. Those who resist all blandishments to "join," whether it be from the commercial adventurers or the good-fellowship boys, may refuse to make the Christian acceptance simply because it is not an individual acceptance alone. They see, rightly, that it requires submission to certain rules and practices, as well as a special degree of sharing with people to whom they would be attracted by no natural affection. Christians seem to them to be no better than the chronic joiners who proudly wave their "membership cards" from the football pool. And perhaps Christianity seems to be specially pernicious since it demands changes in every aspect of life, even the most intimate. It seems to militate against that life-worship which has sustained many thinkers in their struggle with recurring evidence of the beast in man.

It is in fact partly the fault of Christians who have shown more concern for prohibitions than for positive duties. It is a great and sad irony that Christianity, which in every way is the most affirmative of religions, which rests its claims on a supreme sanctifying of human nature in the flesh, should so often have shown itself a cold and miserable thing. Many years ago I was given in the street an evangelical tract which bore the text, "I have a message from God unto thee." When this seemingly very proper title is traced to its biblical source, it proves to be the words spoken by Ehud to King Eglon of Moab, just before stabbing him in a treacherous manner. The misapplication is an unwitting symbol of the way in which many people have been led to regard Christianity. It seems indeed to be the religion with the knife beneath the cloak, striking at all normal joys under the guise of morality. The greater texts like the words of Christ—"I am come that they might have life, and that they might have it more abundantly"—are too readily forgotten. Christians have a perverted genius for making their faith seem at once too easy and too difficult. The continual striving, the doubt which leads believers forward all the time, these are submerged in a bland assurance that one declaration of being converted means that there will never again be anything to worry about. At the same time, commandments are rigidly invoked not only to proscribe wrong-doing but to inhibit the fullness of living. Atheists consistently misinterpret Christianity, but Christians are sometimes not far behind them in so doing.

The Christian must go on living in this world, more fully aware than any other kind of man about what it all means. Everything in his life should become more intense, as he tries to progress, year by year, day by day, hour by hour, toward the glory of God by whom all was created and all is sustained. He cannot live en-

tirely to please himself: but who can? He has to refrain
from following some of his instincts: but who does not?
Life in society imposes restraint, and it is nonsense to
suppose that anyone can do exactly as he pleases. Those
who refuse to submit to Christian restrictions have
already surrendered a good deal of liberty for the sake of
living under fairly civilized conditions with their fellow
men. The "complete man," if he could ever exist, would
be a most unhappy creature and a great nuisance to
everyone else. There is nothing more depressing than
following every inclination and indulging every whim,
without thought for others. This is not a particularly
Christian fact, though the Christian's duty of love guides
him when inclination and self-sacrifice conflict. The
Christian life is directed toward God, conscious of de-
privation until the will is attuned to his.

This is where the resistance to Christianity is often
built up, and this is also where the resistance can be
overcome. The unbeliever says, with a degree of impatience, that the Christian may claim to have a magic
thread that will lead him to the heart of the labyrinth,
whatever perils may be encountered on the way. It is
no doubt splendid to know where you are going and
to feel sure of eventual reward and peace. But the love
of the humanist demands something more immediate. It
seems flat and selfish to follow the winding path solely
for what is at the end of it, instead of trying to break
down the walls that separate us from one another. We
hear the sound of many feet and know that there are
other human beings like ourselves who are trying to

tread the same path. Is not our first duty to break through and grasp the warm hands of present life rather than the barren thread that may or may not lead to eternal life? And of course there is truth in this, for the Christian does not follow his appointed path purely for the salvation of his own soul. There is such a thing as keeping oneself too clean when others are pushed into the mud as a result.

It is in the acknowledgment of our common loneliness that we may hope to meet. This is the starting point, where the Christian should be specially ready and able to help. His certainty of a future blessedness should make him more concerned, not less, with the needs of the present. Only those who recognize the loneliness in themselves which no assurance can quite overcome are fit to share the same burden with others. The problem of loneliness is a paradox to the Christian, like that of poverty. In itself it is a blessed state, for it reproduces something fundamental in the earthly life of Christ. Yet it is to be relieved by all means when it is found in other people. It is a feature of human life in which love can always find scope for going to work. Poverty and all that goes with it can be taken away by the exercise of power, even if no love is felt; so that the Christian today often feels himself comparatively at a loss in the face of the large-scale and efficient benevolence which the state can exercise for a variety of motives. But loneliness yields to nothing but an individual act of love. We have looked at the many ways by which people try to flee from it, and have found them all to be wanting.

The act of love is a choice made out of full awareness of the lonely human condition. Without loneliness
there can be no love, since the deepest need can never
be felt. The choice that is made for the sake of greater
personal comfort, even though it may incidentally benefit others, is not a choice of love. It is an unreal choice
unreal because it does not take account of the total
situation in which we live and through which we must
know each other. The Christian who clings to his loneliness and uses it to shut out other people is imperfect
in faith and works alike. There are those who wish
to be solitary within faith: as wrong in their way as
those who flee from society and dwell in the wilderness of pride. I do not speak of those who are truly
called to a hermit's life of continual meditation and in-
tercession, for no man can judge another's vocation.
The danger is with those who inflate their loneliness
and make it a matter between themselves and God only.
It is part of the same pattern which we have seen expressed in so many secular ways. The man who fastens
on his loneliness to the exclusion of others thereby makes
his condition sterile. The more deeply loneliness is realized, the more it should bring understanding of all
humanity. It can be a barrier or a mighty link.

An extremely personalist faith is too common today.
Sometimes it is an excuse for avoiding the more inconvenient religious duties. More often perhaps it is a genuine sense of unworthiness. Other Christians seem much
more certain in their faith. Therefore it is better to
keep apart from them, to leave the public worship of

the church in the hands of the better members. It is just like those in a community who withdraw from activities because they are unwilling to be less than perfect. Christian faith tells us plainly that no one is worthy; it tells us also that all may venture on worthiness. The Lord's Table is not reserved for stained-glass saints, though all who approach it must try to foster the little spark of sainthood that has been implanted in them. It is not a commendable humility which makes people refuse to go to church except when they "feel like going." Christian duty is not feeling but willing. To put off Confirmation until a sense of perfection can be cultivated; to go to church or stay away because of one's attitude to the officiating clergyman; to regard any Christian duty as needing a special favorable moment for its performance: all these are false attitudes. Even excessive scruples about not feeling reverent enough in church can be wrong. The Christian cannot always stop himself from feeling bored; but he can stop himself from being physically absent. Christianity makes a man recognize and accept his lonely condition, but forbids him to cherish it. By calling him to public worship and common fellowship, it does not offer any guaranteed alleviation. The people in the church group may be even more vexing and less humanly attractive than those outside it. What is offered is, simply and yet staggeringly, a way of making loneliness creative; a way of giving, as part of the eternal sacrifice, that inner sorrow which we all must carry wherever we go.

This offer is different from those offers which com-

merce and humanism make to lonely man. We should
be careful about the distinction, for it is too easy to
adopt bad methods toward a good end, thus corrupting
the end itself. There is a danger of driving people into
the arms of the church through fear. Unfortunately, fear
of one kind or another has been used in the past by
organized religion. Fear of eternal punishment, fear of
secular penalties for recusancy, fear of social ostracism
or lack of career advancement, have all helped to account
for numerically large congregations. Fear fills the pews,
and its removal very quickly empties them. If everyone
who did not go to church one Sunday was automatically
struck down by a thunderbolt, the churches would be
full to overflowing, but there would be an end of faith
and an end of Christian love. It would be a devilish irony
if the anxiety and loneliness which have made a gulf
between man and God should operate to drive people
back to religion for the sake of a comfort that should
never be offered. As we shall see, the way of return is
indeed through this desperate human condition. But
churchmen would be as bad as the most unscrupulous
commercial advertisers if they pretended that loneliness
was something that could be dispelled by "joining the
church." If we drag people in solely through crude offers
of fellowship with tea and buns after the service; or if
we play more subtly on psychological fears and offer
an insurance policy not open to non-believers, we are
not doing God's work. The fellowship is a very right
part of Christian belonging; the tea and buns may be
seen as sacramental, if the gospel sacraments have any

true and abiding meaning for us. And it is *meaning*, not escape that Christianity offers, and has offered from the beginning. Contrary to popular belief, the necessary formal rites of becoming a Christian mark the beginning and not the end of real conflict, toil and questioning, always with the assurance that the quest is right to be undertaken and leads somewhere though the road be hard.

This is why Christianity is unpopular today, for we live in an age which likes to have things on easy terms. There are no deferred payments on Christian commitment; the price is absolute—not a surrender of individuality but a radical change which makes one not less but more of a real person. God is not for sale to the highest bidder, and to try to put a price on obedience to his will is the sin of Judas. God promises no minimum wage and no bonus for long service. The reward of his service is absolute for each person, not to be divided or assessed by degrees, for it is nothing less than himself. The whole Christian story is a series of paradoxes that allows no compromise. A man, born in the normal human way as a helpless infant, born as a member of a race whose land was under foreign occupation, condemned and executed while still a young man, yet claims to be God. Whatever we may gain by way of later evidences, the dilemma that faces us today is the dilemma of those who saw Christ in his human incarnation. Though generations of witnesses have testified to the power of Christ in individual lives, though generations of teachers have helped to interpret the most astonishing of all messages, yet the initial scandal remains each time one human soul has to make a decision. It is a choice that demands all or nothing; and the nothing is the abyss of loneliness which is existential fear.

We come before God in fear and trembling. And today perhaps it is not so much that awe in presence of the numinous which filled the Old Testament writers, as terror lest nothing should have meaning, lest nothing indeed should be found really to exist. If Christians, individually or collectively, play on this fear, they are acting in contradiction of the love which should inspire all Christian action. If, however, the Christian acknowledges the same fear in himself, he may the better be able to demonstrate what faith means to him. Since we have to live with our loneliness, that loneliness is absorbed into faith rather than cast out by it. We know that our situation is perilous, anxious, even desperate. But we know also that hope is not lost even though every observable comfort is stripped away. For when we speak of the Holy Spirit as the Comforter, we do not mean the soother who dispenses mass opiates, but the strengthener, the tongue of fire that is never still. Faith means that loneliness is given another dimension, is no longer restricted by the immediate situation within which we seem so hopelessly unable to communicate. For most Christians, anxiety is never quite removed while life in this world continues; but it may be elevated into the means of greater love. We can grasp other hands in the labyrinth, even as our greatest pull is toward the center where all puzzles are made plain. Loneliness is the starting point for the leap in the dark.

1 0

YET NOT ALONE

THERE HAVE been religions and pseudo-religions which have promised to give material benefits to the initiate, to confer on him special wisdom and secret knowledge, to make him invulnerable to the hurts and ills of life. In common with the other great monotheistic religions, Christianity is concerned with invisible and not visible changes. Certainly conversion should be manifested in many visible ways, by a change of conduct and an exercise of love. But there is no guarantee, of the kind promised by secular organizations today, of having no problems once the leap in the dark has been made. The Christian has no magic cloak: the water of baptism cleanses but does not flow into an enchanted moat of defence. It is just as easy to catch cold in a drafty church as in a drafty pub or boxing stadium. The Christian is not set apart from death and suffering, but learns to see them in clearer perspective.

Even spiritual growth is apt to come slowly and with many setbacks. Faith does not usually spring to its full height and strength in a single moment of conversion. Although the blinding illumination that turned Saul to

Paul on the Damascus road is granted to some, for most it is a slower process. Conversion is only the beginning of a new way of life, within which the former externals seem still to operate their power. All that was possessed before is possessed still, but now it has been laid at the feet of Christ and is taken up again only as it may better serve his will. The Christian life is a slow growth into the will of Christ, using every means of Christian discipline to establish a life for which his life is the pattern. It is a continual attention to public and private worship, to study, meditation and proper obedience that may lead at last to a reasonable certainty that right choices are being made. It would no doubt be much easier if everyone were presented at his baptism with a Bible, specially indexed so that an appropriate text could be turned up to solve every imaginable situation in subsequent life. But it is not so: we must struggle on with what illumination we can get, always falling short of perfection yet aiming at nothing less than perfection as the goal. Conscious of mortality, we hope for immortality. Renouncing all rights, we feel the tug of possessiveness. It is through constant tension that we must grow.

Christians may well ask themselves whether this is their image of life, and still more whether it is the image which they present to others. For every Christian is a missionary and a propagandist, so soon as his acquaintances know what faith he professes; and what he does may be of much greater impact than what he writes or says. The public view of the Christian church today is of a structure that is dented but still powerful, split but still holding together on a basis of certain agreed responses to particular questions. It seems to offer a well-knit, though somewhat dull or "square," social life to its members. "Religious people" are to be envied for the consolations they seem to find, even though they find them at the expense of certain pleasures and at the price of a reduced interest in everyday affairs. The thunderings of Bradlaugh are seldom heard today, and people tend instead to look at Christianity with incomprehension and a certain wistfulness. Even its opponents have to admit that the Christian groups have often taken the lead in social work. Though what may in all denominations be described as the Establishment has too often been reactionary, dedicated individuals have seen that their commitment compelled them to alleviate material as well as spiritual afflictions. It may be that the social image of the church, necessary at all times and never more so than during the last century, has grown too powerful. There is always this narrow path to be trodden, which has been mentioned before, between an excess of individualistic piety and an excess of group participation. It may be that the latest tendency is to overstress the latter. Perhaps we have made too much of the tea parties, treasure hunts, the earnest discussions, the rummage sales and bazaars. These indeed we ought to have done and not neglected the other. There would be little of the spirit of Christ in a church group where no friendly word was spoken once the service was over, where the ordinary human activities were not

sanctified and the ordinary human relations not deep-
ened. Yet this is not the whole need. We have attracted
many of the chronic joiners, those who think to flee
from loneliness by not being physically alone. Of them,
too, is the Kingdom of God made. But what if we have
repelled the brave and honest ones who want to ask
really awkward questions? Have Christians committed
the common error of the age, increasing loneliness by
giving solutions which solve nothing?

To some extent the tension between individuals questioning and corporate faith is inevitable. The main-
stream of Christianity flows on with a power that comes
from Christ himself and which makes nonsense or
irrelevance of many of the little side-channels which
single explorers insist on following. There is a right
and necessary distrust of those who claim special knowledge, who are supposed to be the first ever fully to
understand the message of Christ. From Gnostics to
Jehovah's Witnesses, groups of people have been saying
that everybody else is wrong and that there are no other
real Christians in the world but themselves. He who
insists on standing outside the great Christian tradition
may occasionally be a saint with special correctives to
offer, and a few such have been ignored for a long
time and even persecuted. But a heavy burden of proof
is on him, for conversion is conversion into the whole
Body of Christ on earth. It is mediated in an individual
encounter, but it expresses itself in the need for shared
worship and the proper sacraments. Faith grows in and
with the faith of others; the sum of personal decisions

about Christ is to be lived and shown corporately. We have already looked at the dangers of extreme personalism in religion, of holding back until everything "feels right" to the individual judgment.

Yet this is by no means the whole story. To suppose that the situation of the individual has not changed since Christianity was first preached would be to ignore the status of Christianity as a historical as well as a timeless religion. The encounter between God and the individual soul which he has created is out of all bounds of time and space. But its consequences are not so emancipated and they are also a corporate responsibility for the whole body of Christians. For the greater part of recorded history, the situation of man in this world has been a God-ward situation. Some sort of supreme being has been accepted and the need for certain duties and modes of worship has been woven into the framework of society, in spite of private and corporate defections. Now the climate of most countries is secular: in the sense that a man may be considered a reasonable and indeed commendable member of the community, fulfilling all that is required by law and custom, without professing any kind of religious belief. Society organizes its affairs, at local and national levels with the basic secular assumption that there are no supernatural loyalties to be fulfilled. Even in countries where the influence of the church is still strong, there is usually no difficulty in acting as if it did not exist. Christians need by no means regret this unreservedly, since we have seen what perils too much success and power can bring with them.

But it is important to understand the position not only as it affects those who try to serve Christ but those who are newly called to do so. We must try to see the individual in the situation where awareness of Christ first comes upon him, to look at things through his own eyes as they have been conditioned by his environment and upbringing to that moment. It is a situation in which loneliness is seen as inevitable and, by the most clear-sighted and honest, inescapable. All his life, perhaps, he has been lured into joining groups and movements which have promised some release; and every one has proved disappointing. Is this new stirring going to be any better? These words which have been heard so many times before, at compulsory school prayers, in formal civic services, on the lips of "pious" friends—now they seem to make sense for the first time and to speak to him in his lonely condition. But what then: when he turns toward the church that claims to be the guardian and interpreter of these things, does he see a full recognition of the individual who is still battling his way mistily across the frontier? Or does he see only a closed group, where communication is all in one direction and no questions are invited?

It is well known that society today neglects and indeed rejects the individual. Anyone who embarks on so private and yet public a matter as the total acceptance of Christianity finds his way hampered. There is little encouragement for the exercise of individual choice, especially for a choice which is to make the personality new and more individual than ever before. It was said over a hundred years ago—and the accusation strikes even deeper today:

> What does a mere individual count for? Our age knows only too well how little it is, but here also lies the specific immorality of the age. Each age has its own characteristic depravity. Ours is perhaps not pleasure or indulgence or sensuality, but rather a dissolute pantheistic contempt for the individual man.[1]

Everything in this age conspires to throw the individual off balance, to make him feel uncomfortable and unnatural when he recognizes that which is unique to himself. Full reward is given only for participation. And this is where the church—meaning not just a few men armed with ordination papers or a few special enthusiasts, but the whole company of Christian people—really must go in with all flags flying. For it is only in the church that the real meaning both of individuality and of participation may be found. We can go in joyfully, knowing that we have power to transform but not to control, to persuade but not to command. Freed after centuries from the penalties of too much success and its links with the secular power, the church now stands where the church of the Apostles stood. Here we may have lost ground, showing in diminished numbers and emptier churches. But out of the very bleakness which threatens failure, there comes the means of success as Christ would have it and not as the world sees it. Nearly two thousand years ago, a few simple men who had seen the Cross on Calvary set out to turn the world

[1] Søren Kierkegaard, *Concluding Unscientific Postscript* (1846).

upside down. In a society where every established tradition seemed a barrier against them, they proclaimed the startling news that there was no longer any difference, save in external things, between Jew and Gentile, slave and free citizen, man and woman; for they were made one in Jesus Christ, whom they acknowledged to be the Son of God.

That claim, not diminished in the slightest degree, still stands for and through us, who know the Cross not in its physical actuality but through the church which has preached it in good times and in bad. We too can break the barriers that seem unbreakable. If Christ died for all, there is no sense in any sort of grouping which welcomes in the Anglo-American but excludes the Russian, no truth in any mode of thought or action which postulates greater merit in pink skins than in black ones. Not only must the great and obvious divisions disappear. God shows himself in the most trivial aspects of human life, and we must not have our heads so much among the stars that we fail to notice what is happening very close to the ground. The opportunities do not come only in the full light of publicity, when the affairs of nations are being settled or when some big disaster shows where the immediate duty lies. Few can participate in the greatest events, but for all the opportunity is never far away. We shall achieve our aim of making men and women become what they really are, only if we learn to respect the commonplace and the apparently trivial. The chance meeting on a windy corner may have as much significance in God's

purpose as the international conference that is planned
with all the attention of modern publicity. There are
souls to be saved on working days as well as Sundays.
May we vow always to remember the crudity of the
Cross as well as its glory! To all Christians, that which
happened one Sabbath eve on a hill by Jerusalem is the
greatest event in the whole story of our race. It made
little stir at the time: a necessary execution that
threatened to blow up into civil disturbance but even-
tually passed off without incident. We rightly offer
to Christ all that can be made lovely through the art of
men and the riches of his own creation. But that is
not enough, if it makes us forget the importance of the
harsh, rough wood. Each individual need is unique and
is to be served within his own situation, wherever it
impinges upon our own.

We have seen that conditions today make the break-
through specially difficult. The truth of Christianity
never changes, but special emphases are needed from age
to age. Heresies start with the laudable attempt to set
right the balance by stressing some factor which ortho-
doxy has tended to neglect. Though human frailty too
easily tips the balance the other way in the process, it
is always important to see that the eternal nature of
Christian teaching is not obscured by a temporary failure
of presentation. That is why we need to find our noblest
visions today in the loneliness that is our common lot,
acknowledged by Christian and atheist alike. The
desolation, the apartness which each one feels as he
becomes more aware of his unique condition may and

must be the means to draw us all into that fellowship which is the way of truth.

Therefore it is necessary to stress the loneliness which is in Christianity—in the life of Christ on earth and the life of every single Christian. It is an element never forgotten in Christian teaching, but too often played down either to attract or to retain popularity. Christianity without the Cross attracts converts of the type imaged by the seed that fell upon rock, which had no roots and quickly withered. Christianity is to be received with joy and hope, but not with false optimism of the type promulgated in this piece of advice to speakers on radio and television programs in New York:

> Admonitions and training of Christians on cross-bearing, forsaking all else, sacrifices, and service usually cause the average listener to turn the dial. Consoling the bereaved and calling sinners to repentance by direct indictment of the listeners, is out of place. . . . As apostles, can we not extend an invitation, in effect: "Come and enjoy our privilege, meet good friends, see what God can do for you!" [2]

I believe that this kind of thing is not only a perversion of Christian truth but is the least likely way of making any lasting impact today. People have been promised too much, and are wearily disillusioned with broken pledges. We need to show how disappointment and apparent loss are sanctified within Christianity so that they become the grounds of victory. It is the self-limiting of God which makes it possible for us in our turn to approach him. In Christ we can see the utter humility which

[2] Quoted by Whyte, *op. cit.*, p. 418.

claims no special privileges but is content to suffer the extreme penalties of taking on human nature. It was the giving of all, which demands all or else accepts nothing as the response. Christian history begins with the loneliness of an unwanted family, members of an oppressed race and denied even a bed for birth. It proceeds through continual rejection and enmity to the last agony of loneliness and apparent failure. These are the truths which our age needs to grasp, uniting them to its own loss of association, its own anxiety. For tomorrow, the emphasis may need to be different, though it can never be far away from the original experience; but we can deal only with what is here and now.

Who ever knew such loneliness as Christ? When we cry out in our pain at not being accepted and understood as we should wish, that pain is not even a shadow of his. Fully man by choice, he knew all that must be endured by those who walk this earth in flesh. Fully God as well, his sufferings were such that the whole of creation shared in them and benefited by them. Even his special friends, chosen to carry his message throughout the world, constantly failed to understand him. They quarreled about precedence, urged him to use miraculous power against their enemies, insisted on seeing him as a temporal ruler with national limitations. It was only through the loneliness of his withdrawal and apparent failure that they were prepared for the transformation that came upon them after the Resurrection. Before that could be, one of the closest and perhaps potentially best of them was to betray him positively, while the others in various degrees betrayed him negatively by forsaking him after his arrest. Peter, who had been the first to acknowledge his divinity, also denied acquaintance with his humanity. There was not one voice to speak in defence of the Son of Man who was the Son of God at the moment of his condemnation; not one voice but the feeble attempt of a Roman magistrate who loved justice, but feared Caesar, prompted by his wife whose dreams were truer than most men's waking thoughts that terrible night. In the loneliness of death, which is the final assertion of loneliness even in those who have fled from it all their lives, Christ seems to have known even the withdrawal of communication with God, as if to leave nothing of human anguish untouched. Man withdraws himself from God by sin, yet because all are sinners that desolation had to come even into the Godhead itself. It is a great and wonderful mystery; but the questioning of lonely man meets its answer in that other question, "My God, my God, why hast thou forsaken me?"

Although that terrible cry was uttered for the sins and sorrows of the whole world, human wills were still left free to reject both the claim and the liberation of Calvary. Men continued to say, as they say ever more insistently today, "You've got to live your own life—no one else can live it for you." They demand actual experience, rejecting all offers that do not come from within the person's own struggle. Modern philosophers, voicing the anxiety of their less articulate contemporaries demand a concrete, particular situation as the basis for judgment. Now since Christianity does claim that all lives find their true meaning only through another which, in its human span, was lived a long time ago, the secular challenge is important. It is the last rock on which our hopes may be founded, or against which they will be shattered. Is human loneliness of such a kind that it allows no real communication, can never be broken through? Or does the full recognition of loneliness give the only key to genuine life? That is the question toward which the present-day situation continually leads, and anyone who is not prepared to abandon humanity to nihilism must try to answer it.

"You've got to live your own life." In the first place, this is not entirely true. As we have seen, we all live to some extent by and for others. It is possible, of course, that the greater part of humanity has always been mistaken in this. It may be that love of the family is unnatural, that attachment to friends is wrong, that any kind of loyalty is misplaced and any sense of fellowship a delusion. It may be; but what we have seen of the self-appointed solitary has not encouraged us to place a great deal of reliance on him. One of the few things which modern fragmented individuals seem to have in common is their need to reach out from loneliness and accept the sacrifices as well as the privileges of shared living. We have seen also that human love never completely overcomes the problem, but that it comes very near to a solution. Apart from that, some degree of sharing is an integral part of the actual situation within which modern thinkers demand that we should make our judgments. If a man is his true self when he judges thus, his real identity derives partly from others who make him what he is at that moment. It is a great deal less, or more, than human to cast off all affections and loyalties so easily.

The Christian answer, however, goes a great deal further than this. Thus challenged, we can offer no compromise by a convenient twisting of words to suit the situation. Instead there is only the perpetual scandal, the stumbling block for all who want the way to be plain and clear throughout. The Christian church teaches precisely what the modern temper denies. It thrusts man right up against the rough wood of the Cross, as it has always done. The choice is his: to assert the rightness of modernity and turn away, or to realize that his feet had strayed until then and that this gallows is no stumbling block but the first step toward real freedom. Life is made genuine only through Christ, in whom all human lives find their meeting point and their place of rest. This is the answer to the question, "What need of Christ?" asked by many who accept the power and truth of Christian teaching but fall back from the unique and seemingly extravagant claims that go with it. Because God took on human nature, and lived a human life and died a human death, all lives have their real center in him.

The doctrine of the Ascension, and the way it is based on narratives in the New Testament, can cause a great deal of puzzlement. There are many Christians who would like to modify it, because it seems to rest on a belief about the structure of the universe which is, to say the least, old-fashioned. Unbelievers can have a great deal of honest fun at the expense of a creed which apparently asks us to affirm that heaven has a spatial location somewhere in the sky above the region of Jerusalem but that is to make heavy prose out of poetry —and not human poetry, which is expendable. This is God's own poetry, his way of making the Apostles understand what had happened: that Christ's body was indeed restored to life and not decaying in the tomb; that it has been freed of the material limitations of bodies which had not passed from death to resurrection, and which Christ had been willing previously to accept; that the life of Christ on earth was nevertheless done; that his presence, real and recognizable as ever, would be watching over them and guiding them. It was a powerful symbol, but not a "mere" symbol, eligible for periodic revision; it was what they really saw. And the point of it was that the Ascension is in fact the consummation of Christ's mission and that it expresses what people today most desperately need to know. Our human nature is even now glorified in the eternal presence of God. Yes, not just forgiven and redeemed and encouraged, which is wonder enough, but actually glorified. Because that one body was tormented and broken and killed, something has been allowed to happen that gives mankind a status which we may think that no other of God's creatures has ever reached. This very human condition which makes us want to despair is in fact our greatest glory. The hands that we have longed so much to clasp as we stumbled through the labyrinth reach out to us. They are reassuringly human; rough, workman's hands that can draw us out of the darkness where we seem to drown. They are hands that are forever spread to intercede for us, and they are cruelly wounded with nails.

This is our glory. We know that our common lot is to share in the weaknesses and inconveniences of humanity. We know only too well the grubbiness, the failures, the constant resolves to do better which never seem to reach their mark. Above all, we know that to be alive is to be mortal and that there is no certainty like the certainty of death. We know that every situation carries its own destruction with it, since it is realized in time and begins to pass away from the moment we become aware of it. Many have thought that conscious preparation for death is the highest to which we can attain in this life. But understanding all this, we may understand also the hope and the splendor of the human condition. This very human body, which we so often hate yet which is our only means of consciousness and communication here on earth, is acceptable to God not only by reason of his creation but by reason of his suffering.

Yet this lifting of the burden is not to be regarded as a lifting of responsibility. As we face the apparent dilemma of Christianity, we see that either fear or hope of losing the personal decision is unjustified. Choice is still demanded of every man and choice is unique within his situation. If there should be any doubt about Christian responsibility it can be resolved, as most of such doubts can, by reference to the record of the Gospels. Christ spoke to each individual who came to him, judging the situation and commanding what was necessary for that individual at that moment of decision. Some were to leave all and follow him, others were to go back to their daily routine in full awareness of the new power that had come into their lives. Throughout history, the Christian has been required to attend to the voice that calls him and to fulfill the message that is for all men and yet uniquely for him. This, too, is part of the paradox and scandal of Christianity: that an absolute standard is given, yet every individual life must fit within it in a special way. Choice remains free, and the Christian choice is authentic to the extent that it is directed toward the will of Christ as it stands for each one of us here and now. On whatever ground we judge the moment of choice, we must agree in seeing it as part of the total situation; and that situation includes awareness of the Christ-event. Even for those who deny it and flee from it, that event reveals an attitude of acceptance or rejection in every decision that is made.

Yet how is man today, lonely, frightened, uncertain, to approach the pattern of Christ? To keep his commandments and take part in the corporate worship of his church is a minimum of obedience, and may seem to be little more than one among many possible commitments with which we are assailed from every side. What has Christianity to offer that is specially valid for this age of anxiety and loneliness? Has the message which has called forth heroic virtues in every generation ceased to communicate in our present predicament? The answer may be, as it always has been, at the heart of the Christian mystery and in the way which has caused the gravest offence. Many people have seen difficulty and even something repellent in the idea of atonement. It has seemed to be an abnegation of individual responsibility, an attempt to escape from individual guilt. Yet what Christianity plainly teaches is that Christ died for the sins of the whole world, and that individual responsibility is not lessened but heightened by this great fact. To put it in the simplest terms, human sin becomes much more serious by the very fact that God has thus acted to relieve its burden. Or if we may venture to speak in human terms—and such boldness is permitted by the fact of the Incarnation—we do not feel that an act of kindness that springs from love is to be an excuse for not caring what we do next. We all know how human love and forgiveness make us feel humbly resolved to improve on conduct which has led to the loved one being hurt. We know that every acceptance of human love is an increase of responsibility and a sharpening of choice. How then shall we say that the divine love manifested on the Cross takes away the need for individual choice? Further, what can we do to show that love working effectively in our lives as we develop them on earth?

The answer, if we can dare to grasp it, is also the answer to the problem of loneliness. We can make the great Atonement an increase of personal guilt if we choose to regard it as something objective which makes all our own actions a matter of indifference. To understand what it really means, we must try to incorporate it into our own lives. Is human loneliness so complete that no communication is possible and each of us must live forever in isolation? Christ has shown us that this is not so; we can in fact break through and help to share the burden that can never be entirely lifted. One of the great words of the New Testament is that which is rendered in the Authorized Version as *compassion*: "suffering with others." We are told many times how Christ had compassion on the suffering ones who came to him. The Greek word suggests a feeling that troubles the inward parts; as we might say colloquially of a tragic event, "It really turned me over inside." It is the feeling which the Samaritan is related to have had for the wounded traveler, after the priest and the Levite had viewed his distress objectively and failed to take it into their own lives. It is through suffering with others that we may hope to show that we are greater than our loneliness.

Christians are accustomed to the idea of seeing their sufferings as united with the sufferings of Christ, offering them to him as part of their gratitude and humility for the Atonement. Since that Atonement was made for all mankind, we can play our part by accepting some of the burden. The attempt may lead us into some strange experiences, as we try to transcend time and space by awareness of our unity with others. If we cannot change the past, we may be able to change its meaning. If there are hands that we cannot grasp directly, we may yet touch them through the wounded hands that link us all. The more we try to flee from loneliness, the more tightly it holds us. If it can be accepted not as a personal misfortune but as a necessary consequence of being committed to unique experience and unique choice, it can become the way of love and compassion. It is no great flight of mysticism to interpret the exhortation, "Bear ye one another's burdens" more fully than in the basic and important way of doing material good as the opportunity offers. We are all so deeply involved with one another that every bit of sorrow and suffering is communicated to all. We may try to see our own trouble not as a special misfortune to be groaned over and cherished in self-pity but as a part of the human situation which is redeemed and glorified above any of its possible merits. A Teutonic chief who heard the Christian story long ago swore that, if he and his warriors had been present on Calvary, Christ would not have had to suffer and die. But Christ did suffer and die, and our human existence which he took upon him means that we were all in fact there at the foot of the Cross. Instead of sighing that we would like to have been able to save Christ there in the flesh, we may ponder what we can do since he in fact saved us. When we share the sufferings of another, we are doing what he did for every one of us. His sacrifice was unique and divine; every human sacrifice is thereby made meaningful.

Therefore our duty is not complete if we feel sorry only for those who are bound to us by special affection.

Sympathy for the immediate case, where something definite can be done, will be heightened if we extend sympathy also to the unseen and the unknown. It is through suffering that we understand each other. It is suffering which teaches us that we are lonely, yet not alone. The shadow of mortality which hangs over our earthly path is a link in our humanity, and is overcome when we realize this. Since our sins have been borne, we are to bear the sins of others and make a humble sacrifice of the many ways in which they trouble us. By so doing, we may learn not to judge others, not indeed to speak about sin at all except in connection with our own actions. If we try to understand, we may appreciate what it really means to be ourselves forgiven. The harm that others do us can easily become an embittering thing if we allow it, increasing the loneliness which holds us apart. Or it can make us see more clearly the meaning of the harm we do to others, and so destroy the barriers with a lightening flood of sympathy. Are we inconvenienced by an industrial strike, occasioned by some minor dispute that seems nothing more than a childish display of temper? Let us think of the generations who worked in dreadful conditions because men's hearts were hardened by the touch of gold. Let us offer the slight frustration of the moment in reparation for all those who once were afraid to speak out lest they and their families should starve. Are we irritated by the behavior of children who seem to lack any discipline? Let us remember the millions of children who have suffered under cruel rules until all their spontaneity was crushed. It is thus that we may share in all ages, being free of the question whether things have been steadily getting better or worse.

Every attempt to flee from loneliness is doomed to failure. By recognizing loneliness as an inevitable part of the human condition, we may yet transcend it. That which seems most to separate us from our fellow men proves at last to be the strongest factor uniting us. We are truly members one of another, not by any external act of "joining" but by willingly accepting and making positive our share in the sum of human sorrow. We rightly feel satisfaction in the great achievements of the human race; let us accept the same involvement in its failure and its guilt. We are all guilty, not only of actual individual sins but of the cruelties and injustices which men and women have practiced on each other since history began. When we stood at the foot of the Cross, it was not to attempt to save Christ by some heroic deed; it was to mock and deride him as his human strength faded under the load that no mere man could bear for us. The crime is repeated every time a sentient creature is hurt in any way, and each of us is present wherever it may be. When we realize this guilt our loneliness seems to be intensified. But the crime brought pardon, and taught us how we, too, may forgive. The only true belonging lies in the fact of being human and living as creatures of God. There is no fee but the struggle of birth, and no dismissal save in death. And when we seem to leave, it is only the beginning.

BOOK LIST

The following books will be useful to readers who wish further to study particular aspects of the subject.

John Baillie	*The Belief in Progress*
William Bartlett	*Irrational Man*
H. J. Blackham	*Six Existential Thinkers*
C. S. Lewis	*The Four Loves*
Walter Lowrie	*Kierkegaard*
Leslie Paul	*The Annihilation of Man*
David Riesman	*The Lonely Crowd*
Paul Roubiczek	*The Misinterpretation of Man*
Paul Tournier	*Escape from Loneliness*
William H. Whyte	*The Organization Man*

Type used in this book
Body, 10 on 13 and 9 on 10 Janson
Display, Janson
Paper: GM Antique